macOS App Development: The SwiftUI Way

Grace Huang

macOS App Development: The SwiftUI Way

Grace Huang

ISBN 9798877075795

Contents

CONTENTS

First Edition: December 2022

Second Edition: January 2024

Introduction

Introduced in 2019, SwiftUI is a user interface toolkit that allows you to create applications with the power of the Swift programming language for all Apple platforms, including iOS, macOS, tvOS, watchOS, and even the newest visionOS.

Before the launch of SwiftUI, developers had to use platform-specific UI frameworks to develop user interfaces; for example, AppKit for macOS apps, TVUIKit for tvOS, and WatchKit for watchOS apps. SwiftUI became the unified UI framework for building user interfaces for all Apple devices.

This book will primarily focus on building macOS apps with SwiftUI, covering both coding and releasing apps. Some details for releasing apps on different platforms (iOS, macOS, tvOS, watchOS and visionOS) may differ, so a single focus on macOS development aims to bring more clarity and avoid confusion.

The book will also touch upon the basics of SwiftUI, which can potentially be applied to other platforms.

End Goal

By the end of this book, you should be able to create macOS apps independently and publish them to your users.

Structure

> "Learning is an active process. We learn by doing. Only knowledge that is used sticks in your mind." — Dale Carnegie, "How to Stop Worrying and Start Living"

In light of this guiding principle by Dale Carnegie, this book prioritizes doing and then goes into the details later.

The book is structured into 4 parts. Each part consists of multiple chapters.

Part 1

The first part is getting you ready for the development:

- Chapter 1: Getting Started

Part 2

The second part is a walkthrough of multiple macOS projects. It guides you to create these applications from scratch, from easy to hard, using SwiftUI.

The chapters are:

- Chapter 2: Building A Number Randomizer
- Chapter 3: Building A Windowless Screenshot App
- Chapter 4: Building A Photo Fetching App
- Chapter 5: Building A Note-taking App

Part 3

The third part is a deep dive into macOS development and SwiftUI basics. Why place the part of basics after the projects? It is counter-intuitive, but we learn better by doing first (building the projects). You may have questions along the way. This part will be the place to answer them in detail.

- Chapter 6: macOS Development and SwiftUI Basics

Part 4

The fourth part is about preparation for the app release.

- Chapter 7: Preparing For Launch
- Chapter 8: App Store
- Chapter 9: Self-Distribution

Prerequisites

In addition to this book, you will also need the following to follow along:

- A Mac computer capable of running Xcode
- Internet access
- Enrollment in the Apple Developer Program, which costs 99 USD.

Assumptions

Basic Programming Skills

This book assumes you are new to macOS app development with SwiftUI, not necessarily new to programming in general. If you have prior programming experience in other languages, it should be easier to follow the steps in the book.

Use SwiftUI, But Not Focus On Swift

The book focuses on using SwiftUI to build macOS apps but does not delve deep into the Swift language. Throughout the book, tips for Swift will be mentioned.

Xcode Version 15

The latest Xcode version at the time of writing is 15, which was publicly released on September 18, 2023. All examples and screenshots are based on Xcode 15.

If you have earlier or later Xcode versions, expect some differences. I will try my best to update the book over time.

Swift 5

All code in this book is written in Swift 5. If you build your project with an earlier or later Swift Language Version, expect some differences.

Getting Book Updates

I will do my best to keep the book up to date with the latest versions of Xcode and SwiftUI. To receive the latest updates on the book, subscribe to my mailing list by sending an email to higracehuang@gmail.com, including 1) **the book name** and 2) **the platform where you purchased it**.

Code Examples

You can get a copy of the source code https://github.com/higracehuang.

Suggestions

Your feedback will always be appreciated. If anything is unclear or if there are typos in this book, please feel free to contact me via any of the following ways:

- **Email**: higracehuang@gmail.com
- **X/Twitter**: https://x.com/imgracehuang
- **LinkedIn**: https://www.linkedin.com/in/lghuang/

Ready? Now, let's cut to the chase!

Chapter 1: Getting Started

If you've done iOS development in the past, the steps discussed in this chapter will be very similar. Feel free to skip this chapter and move on to the next!

Mac Computer

You can use a regular MacBook, MacBook Air, or iMac to develop a macOS app. It doesn't matter.

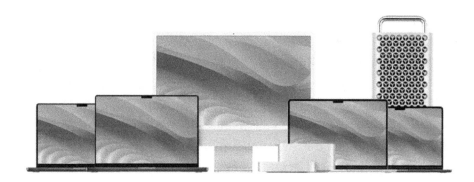

Figure 1. Computers suitable for macOS development

However, newer models may have more powerful processors, resulting in a dramatic reduction in build times and faster development on Xcode.

Install Xcode

1. Open the App Store on your Mac.
2. Use the search bar in the top-right corner and type Xcode.
3. Click on the Xcode app in the search results.

4. On the Xcode app page, click the Get button to download and install it.
5. You may be prompted to enter your Apple ID credentials to complete the installation.
6. Once the installation is complete, find Xcode in your Applications folder.

Keep in mind that Xcode is a large application, so the download and installation process may take some time depending on your internet connection speed.

While waiting, treat yourself to a cup of coffee or tea. You deserve it!

Apple Developer Program Membership

To develop macOS or iOS apps, you'll need to enroll in the **Apple Developer Program**. Membership includes access to beta OS releases, advanced app capabilities, and tools needed to develop, test, and distribute apps. At the time of writing, it costs $99 for individuals and organizations per year.

You might wonder, if you're not ready to publish this app to the App Store, do you still need to pay $99 immediately? The answer is no. You can build it on your Mac computer. However, once you're ready to release, you'll need to be in the program.

Tip: Did you know you can develop multiple apps (both macOS and iOS) with the $99 per year? Even though this upfront cost may seem high to some, you can get more benefits from this program if you plan to develop multiple apps. There is *no specific limit* mentioned for the number of apps that can be uploaded under a single developer account.

To sign up for the Apple Developer Program:

1. Visit https://developer.apple.com/.
2. Click "Account" to sign in or create an Apple ID.
3. Choose your developer program type (Individual or Company).
4. Fill out the enrollment form, agree to terms, and submit.
5. If required, enter payment details.
6. Wait for Apple's approval.
7. Once approved, access resources, download Xcode, and submit apps.

Chapter 2: Building A Number Randomizer

Difficulty Level: **Easy**

To begin the journey of building a macOS app, let's start with something simple, so you know building such an app is not that intimidating!

For the first project, we will build an app to generate random numbers. Here's a sneak peek at the app we'll be creating:

Figure 2. The macOS app

Throughout the development of this app, we'll gain familiarity with:

- The process of building a macOS app
- Basics of SwiftUI

Requirements for This App

This app needs to have the following features:

- **Generate Random Numbers**: Implement a mechanism to generate random numbers within the range of 1 to 100.
- **Button**: Include a button that, when pressed, generates a random number within the range.

Creating a New SwiftUI Project

1. Open Xcode app.

- On the left pane, you have a few options for starting a project.
- On the right pane are the existing projects.

Assuming this is the new time you are using Xcode, the right pane should be empty.

Let's choose the option Create New Project....

Figure 3. Create New Project

2. Choose macOS in the top menu, and choose App in Application.

3. Create a macOS project named `NumberRandomizer`.

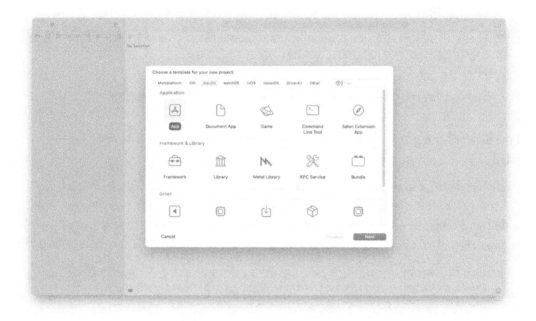

Figure 4. Create macOS App

4. Enter the `Product Name`.

In this example, we will just simply call it `NumberRandomizer`.

5. Select `Team`.

If you've enrolled in the Apple Developer Program, you can choose your team. If not, you can choose `None` for now. Before you publish the app, you will need to join the Apple Developer Program.

Enrolling in the Apple Developer Program beforehand is recommended.

6. Enter the `Organization Identifier`.

In this example, we will use `com.deelightfullabs.`, which is the identifier that I use. **You should have a unique identifier for your project.**

As you type it, you can quickly notice the Bundle Identifier is formed as `com.deelightfullabs.NumberRandomizer`.

Tip: A `Bundle Identifier` is used to identify this particular app. An `Organization Identifier` is used to identify the company or individual that develops this project.

For example, for the Screenshot app in macOS developed by Apple, the `Bundle Identifier` is `com.apple.screencapture`. In this case, the `Organization Identifier` is `com.apple`. The `Project Name` is `screencapture`.

7. Choose `SwiftUI` as `Interface`, and `Swift` as the `Language`.

Tip: Swift is the programming language we are using to build the app. Before Swift was the main programming language, it was Objective-C.

Swift has a simpler syntax than Objective-C. According to an article by Fast Company[1], when the second largest ride-sharing company Lyft rewrote the iOS code from Objective-C to Swift, the code base size went down to less than a third of the original size.

Swift also offers better memory management. As stated by Apple, Swift is 2.6 times faster than Objective-C.

SwiftUI is a whole set of tools that gives us images, buttons, form elements, and many other common UI controls. With all these tools, SwiftUI creates a piece of UI, called `View`.

8. Choose `None` for `Storage`.

We don't need to store data in this project. Later in the book, we will touch upon the `Storage` for other use cases.

9. Click `Next`.

---

[1]https://www.fastcompany.com/3050266/lyft-goes-swift-how-and-why-it-rewrote-its-app-from-scratch-in-apples-new-lang

Figure 5. App Information

10. Choose the directory under which you would like to save the project.

Figure 6. App Location

Make sure to turn on `Create Git repository on my Mac`. A git local repository will be initialized when the project is created.

11. Click `Create` to finally create the project.

Xcode generates the code for a basic macOS app with necessary boilerplates for you, and starts to build the project as soon as it is created.

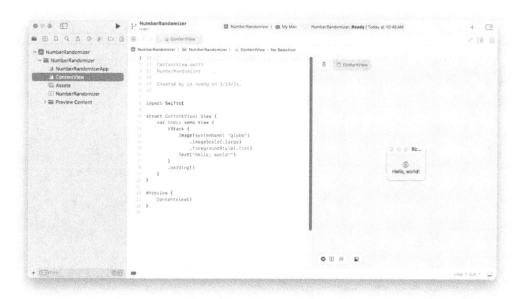

As you can see in the snapshot above:

- On the left pane, it shows the file structure of the project.

  - NumberRandomizerApp: This Swift file represents the main structure of your Xcode project. It contains the primary code and configurations for your app.
  - ContentView: This file typically contains the main SwiftUI view of your app. It defines the structure and layout of the user interface.
  - NumberRandomizer Entitlements: This file may include entitlements for your app, specifying permissions and capabilities it has on the device.
  - Assets: This is where you can store and organize any image assets or media files used in your app.

- On the right pane (called Canvas), it is the preview of the app, where Xcode offers a live representation of the user interface, allowing developers to visualize and interact with design changes in real-time.
- The middle pane shows the generated code, with ContentView shown.

At this point, the code we have so far is also committed to your local git history.

Playing With the Starter App

1. Click the ▶ button on the top left pane of Xcode, to run the app.

Tip: Throughout the book, we will frequently mention running the app by clicking the ▶ button, to verify no build errors.

If you chose None for Team when you were creating the app, you may see this warning. In this case, choose Open Anyway because you are the developer at this moment.

Once the build is complete, you will see a functioning app, like this:

In this app, you can see the following elements:

- A globe-like icon
- A welcoming line of text saying "Hello, World!"

Congratulations! You've successfully created a macOS app.

Diving Deep into `ContentView` code

In Xcode, click to open `ContentView.swift`.

```
1   import SwiftUI
2
3   struct ContentView: View {
4       var body: some View {
5           VStack {
6               Image(systemName: "globe")
7                   .imageScale(.large)
8                   .foregroundStyle(.tint)
9               Text("Hello, world!")
10          }
11          .padding()
```

```
12          }
13      }
14
15      #Preview {
16          ContentView()
17      }
```

Let's break it down and take a look at how it works.

Preview

In this file, you can see two distinct structs: ContentView and Preview.

```
1      struct ContentView: View {
2          ...
3      }
```

The ContentView struct describes the content and layout that the app will rely on.

```
1      #Preview {
2          ContentView()
3      }
```

The Preview struct describes how to show the preview (a.k.a., Canvas) on the right pane for ContentView. It is very helpful during development: whenever the view is updated, without running the app, you can easily see what it looks like in the Preview.

Here are a few things about the Preview:

- When the app is running, it does not execute the Preview at all.
- If you prefer not to use the preview, you can simply remove the Preview struct.
- You can have multiple previews for one view.

SwiftUI: Visual Building Blocks

Let's take a closer look at the ContentView.

```
1   struct ContentView: View {
2       var body: some View {
3           VStack {
4               Image(systemName: "globe")
5                   .imageScale(.large)
6                   .foregroundStyle(.tint)
7               Text("Hello, world!")
8           }
9           .padding()
10      }
11  }
```

Here is the breakdown of the code:

- `struct ContentView: View`: This declares a structure named `ContentView` that conforms to the `View` protocol. In SwiftUI, views are the fundamental building blocks of the user interface.
- `var body: some View`: This is a computed property named `body`, which returns a view. The `some View` syntax indicates that the type returned by `body` is a specific type conforming to the `View` protocol, but it doesn't specify the exact type explicitly.
- `VStack { ... }`: This is a vertical stack (`VStack`) container that arranges its child views vertically.
- `Image(systemName: "globe")`: This creates an image view using the system symbol named "globe." System symbols are part of the SF Symbols library provided by Apple.
- `.imageScale(.large)`: This modifies the image view to use a large scale. It adjusts the size of the symbol image.
- `.foregroundStyle(.tint)`: This sets the foreground color style of the image view to the default tint color. The tint color is often used to adapt to the app's accent color.
- `Text("Hello, world!")`: This adds a text view with the string `"Hello, world!"`.
- `.padding()`: This adds padding around the entire `VStack`, ensuring some space between the content and the container's edges.

So, in summary, this SwiftUI code creates a simple view hierarchy with an image (globe icon) and a text view arranged vertically in a stack. The image is customized to have a larger scale and use the default tint color. The entire content is then padded for a visually pleasing layout.

Creating the Main User Interface

With the above understanding of the starter app, we can create our NumberRandomizer app on top of it.

1. Remove the original code.

First, let's delete the original UI code:

- Remove the Image, and the Text, because we don't need it any more.
- Keep the VStack, because our UI still uses it to verically structure the elements.

After the clean-up, the ContentView will look like the following:

```
import SwiftUI

struct ContentView: View {
    var body: some View {
        VStack {

        }
        .padding()
    }
}

#Preview {
    ContentView()
}
```

2. Display the number.

Add the display of the number into the UI, by using Text():

```
1   import SwiftUI
2
3   struct ContentView: View {
4       var body: some View {
5           VStack {
6               Text("?")
7           }
8           .padding()
9       }
10  }
11
12  #Preview {
13      ContentView()
14  }
```

For now, a question mark ? is shown by default.

3. Add a button named "Generate Random Number"

Incorporate the following button setup into the ContentView.

```
1   Button {
2
3   } label: {
4       Text("Generate Random Number")
5   }
```

The ContentView will look like this:

```
1   struct ContentView: View {
2       var body: some View {
3           VStack {
4               Text("?")
5               Button {
6
7               } label: {
8                   Text("Generate Random Number")
9               }
10          }
```

```
11          .padding()
12      }
13  }
```

4. Run the app.

Figure 7. The NumberRandomizer app

Clicking the button currently doesn't trigger any action, as expected. We need to add click logic: when the button is clicked, display a random number in the Text element.

Adding the Click Logic

1. Add a @State variable to keep track of the random number.

```
1   @State private var randomNum: Int?
```

The @State property wrapper in SwiftUI is used to declare a state variable within a SwiftUI view. State variables are used to store and manage the data that can change over time, influencing the appearance and behavior of the user interface. We will delve into the details of @State in Chapter 6.

In the given code above, `@State private var randomNum: Int?` declares a state variable named randomNum of type `Int?` (an optional integer). The private keyword ensures that the state variable is only accessible within the scope of the containing view.

After adding the `@State` variable, the `ContentView` looks like this:

```
1   import SwiftUI
2
3   struct ContentView: View {
4     @State private var randomNum: Int?
5
6     var body: some View {
7       VStack {
8         Text("?")
9         Button {
10
11        } label: {
12          Text("Generate Random Number")
13        }
14      }
15      .padding()
16    }
17  }
18
19  #Preview {
20    ContentView()
21  }
```

2. Display the random number when it becomes available.

In the `Text()` view, it will check whether the `randomNumber` is available. If yes, it will show the value; otherwise, it will show "?".

```
1   Text(randomNum != nil ? "\(randomNum!)" : "?")
```

With this change, the `ContentView` looks like this:

```
1   import SwiftUI
2
3   struct ContentView: View {
4     @State private var randomNum: Int?
5
6     var body: some View {
7       VStack {
8         Text(randomNum != nil ? "\(randomNum!)" : "?")
9         Button {
10
11        } label: {
12          Text("Generate Random Number")
13        }
14      }
15      .padding()
16    }
17  }
18
19  #Preview {
20    ContentView()
21  }
```

3. Update the random number when the button is clicked.

Below is the logic for generating a random number between 1 and 100.

```
1   randomNum = Int.random(in: 1...100)
```

Add the code for generating a random number inside the button handler; the ContentView looks like this:

```
1   import SwiftUI
2
3   struct ContentView: View {
4     @State private var randomNum: Int?
5
6     var body: some View {
7       VStack {
8         Text(randomNum != nil ? "\(randomNum!)" : "?")
9         Button {
10          randomNum = Int.random(in: 1...100)
11        } label: {
12          Text("Generate Random Number")
13        }
14      }
15      .padding()
16    }
17  }
18
19  #Preview {
20    ContentView()
21  }
```

4. Run the app.

Upon clicking the button, a new random number is displayed in the UI.

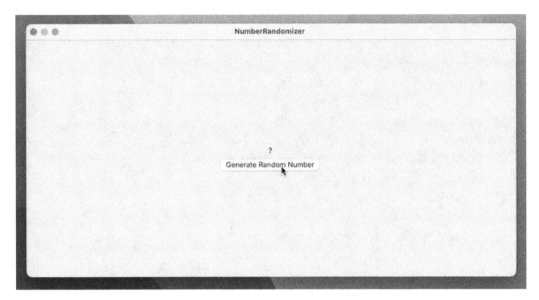

Figure 8. The NumberRandomizer app

Nice job! The core functionality is complete.

Styling the UI

Now, let's style the UI to make it cleaner and more user-friendly.

  1. Style the text.

We would like to make the text for displaying the random number bigger
(`.font(.system(size: 30))`) so that it is easy to see, and also add some space
(`.padding()`) next to the button.

```
1  Text(randomNum != nil ? "\(randomNum!)" : "?")
2    .font(.system(size: 30))
3    .padding()
```

  2. Style the button.

We would also like to make the button bigger (`.font(.system(size: 20))`) and
add some space (`.padding()`) next to it.

```
1   Button {
2     randomNum = Int.random(in: 1...100)
3   } label: {
4     Text("Generate Random Number")
5       .padding()
6       .font(.system(size: 20))
7   }
```

With both of the changes, the ContentView looks like this:

```
1   import SwiftUI
2
3   struct ContentView: View {
4     @State private var randomNum: Int?
5
6     var body: some View {
7       VStack {
8         Text(randomNum != nil ? "\(randomNum!)" : "?")
9           .font(.system(size: 30))
10          .padding()
11        Button {
12          randomNum = Int.random(in: 1...100)
13        } label: {
14          Text("Generate Random Number")
15            .padding()
16            .font(.system(size: 20))
17        }
18      }
19      .padding()
20    }
21  }
22
23  #Preview {
24    ContentView()
25  }
```

3. Run the app.

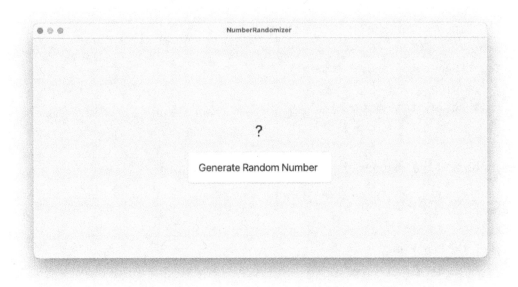

Congratulations! Now we have a functional app for generating random numbers.

Full Code

You can find the full code for this project at https://github.com/higracehuang/NumberRandomizer-xcode15.

If you have any questions, please feel free to reach out by sending me a note at higracehuang@gmail.com.

Potential Future Development

If you are interested, here are a few features that can be added to this project:

- **User Settings**: Allow users to customize the range of random numbers, choose between integers or decimals, or set other preferences.
- **History of Generated Numbers**: Implement a feature that keeps track of previously generated numbers, providing users with a history log.
- **Generate Random Lists**: Extend the app to generate not just single numbers but lists or arrays of random numbers.

Chapter 3: Building A Windowless Screenshot App

Difficulty Level: **Medium**

Now, with the experience of building the app `NumberRandomizer`, you've already learned a lot about macOS apps and SwiftUI.

Let's explore something different to gain insights into other aspects of macOS development: creating a menu bar and interfacing with other apps in the OS.

This is the app that we are going to build:

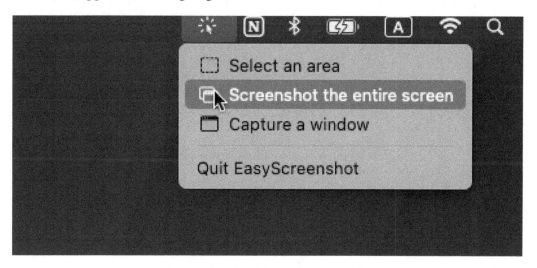

Figure 9. The macOS app EasyScreenshot

By building this app, we will become familiar with:

- Usage of the Status Bar
- How to build a windowless app
- How to interact with native apps on macOS
- Basics of SwiftUI

Requirements For This App

This app needs to have the following features:

- Users can access the functionality via the status bar.
- Users can take screenshots by selecting an area on the screen, a window, or capturing the entire screen.
- No main window is needed.

Creating A macOS App

1. Create a macOS project named EasyScreenshot.

Note that, we choose None for Storage. We don't need Core Data in this project.

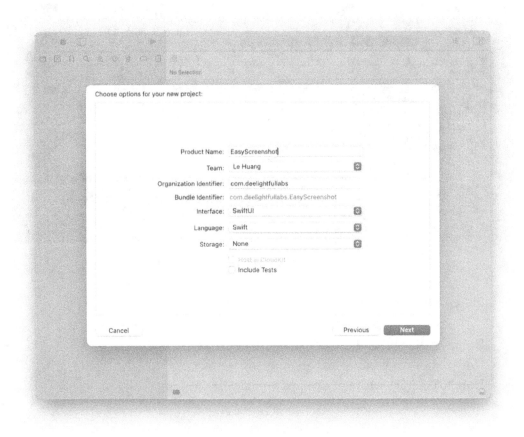

Figure 10. Filling the project information: choose for

2. Check the starter project.

It is a simple app with basic UI.

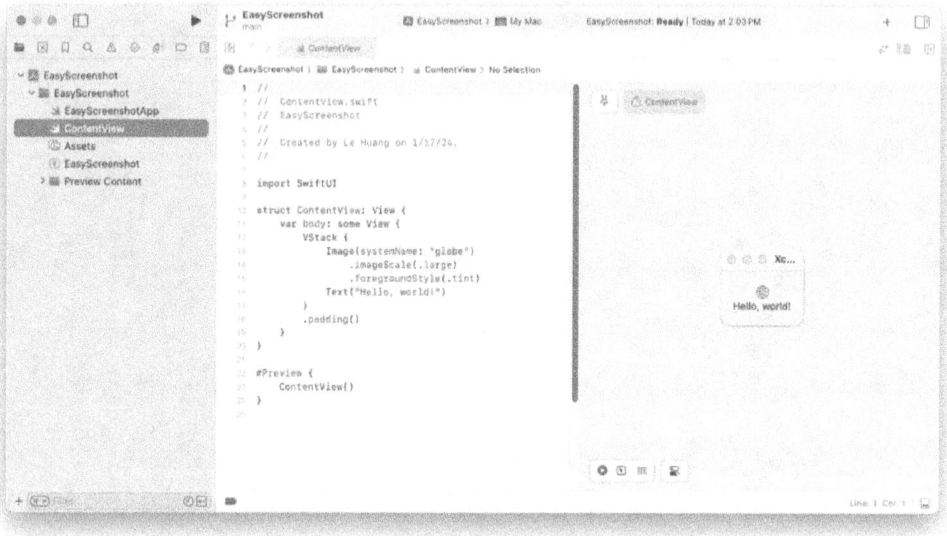

Figure 11. The default code after the project is created.

3. Run the app.

The starter app looks like the following:

Figure 12. What the app looks like when the project is just created.

Creating A Status Bar Icon

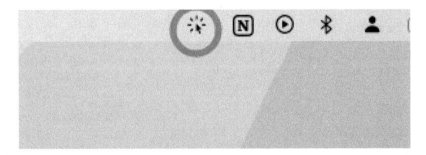

Figure 13. The Status Bar Icon that we are going to create

1. Create a new file called AppDelegate.swift.

Within the new file, set it to show a status item in the menu bar.

In this file, we create a delegate object for the application. What does it mean? It means that when the application reaches a certain state, the Application Delegate will receive notifications.

The most important states are:

- applicationDidFinishLaunching: it is great for startup configuration and construction.
- applicationWillTerminate: it is great for clean-up after the app ends.

In this app, we want to set up a menu in the status bar at the startup time, so applicationDidFinishLaunching is perfect for this case.

The full code of AppDelegate.swift is the following:

```
1   import SwiftUI
2
3   class AppDelegate: NSObject, NSApplicationDelegate {
4     var statusBarItem: NSStatusItem?
5     func applicationDidFinishLaunching(_ notification: Notification) {
6
7       statusBarItem = NSStatusBar.system
8         .statusItem(withLength: NSStatusItem.squareLength)
9       if let statusBarButton = statusBarItem?.button {
10        statusBarButton.image = NSImage(
11          systemSymbolName: "cursorarrow.rays",
12          accessibilityDescription: nil
13        )
14      }
15
16      let mainMenu = NSMenu()
17
18      statusBarItem?.menu = mainMenu
19    }
20  }
```

- An NSStatusItem is created to represent an item in the status bar. The length of the status item is set to NSStatusItem.squareLength, making it a square shape.
- The status item is configured with an image. The image is set to the system symbol named "cursorarrow.rays," representing a cursor arrow with rays. This symbol is used as the icon for the status item in the menu bar.
- An empty NSMenu named mainMenu is created.
- The statusBarItem's menu is set to mainMenu, indicating that the menu will be displayed when the user clicks on the status item in the menu bar.

The code should not take effect at this point because the `AppDelegate` is not wired up with the app.

2. Instantiate `AppDelegate` in `EasyScreenshotApp.swift`.

```
1   import SwiftUI
2
3   @main
4   struct EasyScreenshotApp: App {
5
6       @NSApplicationDelegateAdaptor(AppDelegate.self)
7       private var appDelegate
8
9       var body: some Scene {
10          WindowGroup {
11              ContentView()
12          }
13      }
14  }
```

`@NSApplicationDelegateAdaptor(AppDelegate.self)` integrates the `AppDelegate` class as the delegate for the `NSApplication`, and `private var appDelegate` creates an instance of this delegate within the `EasyScreenshotApp` structure.

This ensures that the `AppDelegate` class handles application-related events for the EasyScreenshot app.

3. Run the app.

You should see an icon like this on the status bar.

Figure 14. The status bar icon

At this moment, it should do nothing yet when you click on it.

Tip Starting from macOS 13.0 (Ventura, released in October 2022), you can leverage MenuBarExtra to effortlessly create a menu in the status bar using SwiftUI, replacing the need for the AppKit framework (e.g., using NSStatusItem and NSImage)

However, in this book, we continue to use Application Delegate, as it is compatible with older OS versions. Also, you can see AppKit also works with SwiftUI, so you can implement parts of your AppKit app in SwiftUI or mix interface elements between the two frameworks.

Tip You may have noticed the class with the prefix NS, and wondered what it means. NS comes from NextSTEP, the original operating system that became Mac OS X when Apple acquired Next.

> Historical Note: If you're wondering why so many of the classes you encounter have an NS prefix, it's because of the past history of Cocoa and Cocoa Touch. Cocoa began life as the collected frameworks used to build apps for the NeXTStep operating system. When Apple purchased NeXT back in 1996, much of NeXTStep was incorporated into OS X, including the existing class names. Cocoa Touch was introduced as the iOS equivalent of Cocoa; some classes are available in both Cocoa and Cocoa Touch, though there are also a large number of classes unique to each platform. Two-letter prefixes like NS and UI (for User Interface elements on iOS) are reserved for use by Apple.

Creating a Menu with multiple menu items.

1. Create an object of NSMenu, and also create several NSMenuItem objects.

In each NSMenuItem object, define the name of the item, the icon, and the action.

```
1   import SwiftUI
2
3   class AppDelegate: NSObject, NSApplicationDelegate {
4     var statusBarItem: NSStatusItem?
5     func applicationDidFinishLaunching(_ notification: Notification) {
6
7       statusBarItem = NSStatusBar.system
8         .statusItem(withLength: NSStatusItem.squareLength)
9       if let statusBarButton = statusBarItem?.button {
10        statusBarButton.image = NSImage(
11          systemSymbolName: "cursorarrow.rays",
12          accessibilityDescription: nil
13        )
14      }
15
16      let mainMenu = NSMenu()
17
18      /// Creating menu item: area capture
19      let itemSelectArea = NSMenuItem(
20        title: "Select an area",
21        action: #selector(Self.actionSelectArea(_:)),
22        keyEquivalent: "")
23      itemSelectArea.image = NSImage(
24        systemSymbolName: "rectangle.dashed",
25        accessibilityDescription: nil
26      )
27      itemSelectArea.target = self
28      mainMenu.addItem(itemSelectArea)
29
30      /// Creating menu item: entire screen capture
31      let itemCaptureEntireScreen = NSMenuItem(
32        title: "Screenshot the entire screen",
33        action: #selector(Self.actionCaptureEntireScreen(_:)),
```

```
34        keyEquivalent: "")
35      itemCaptureEntireScreen.image = NSImage(
36        systemSymbolName: "macwindow.on.rectangle",
37        accessibilityDescription: nil
38      )
39      itemCaptureEntireScreen.target = self
40      mainMenu.addItem(itemCaptureEntireScreen)
41
42      /// Creating menu item: window capture
43      let itemCaptureWindow = NSMenuItem(
44        title: "Capture a window",
45        action: #selector(self.actionCaptureWindow(_:)),
46        keyEquivalent: "")
47      itemCaptureWindow.image = NSImage(
48        systemSymbolName: "macwindow",
49        accessibilityDescription: nil
50      )
51      itemCaptureWindow.target = self
52      mainMenu.addItem(itemCaptureWindow)
53
54      /// Creating a divider
55      mainMenu.addItem(.separator())
56
57      /// Creating menu item:  quit the app
58      let itemQuit = NSMenuItem(
59        title: "Quit EasyScreenshot",
60        action: #selector(self.actionExitApp(_:)),
61        keyEquivalent: "")
62      itemQuit.target = self
63      mainMenu.addItem(itemQuit)
64
65    statusBarItem?.menu = mainMenu
66  }
67
68  @objc private func actionExitApp(_ sender: Any?) {
69    NSApp.terminate(self)
70  }
71
72  @objc private func actionCaptureEntireScreen(_ sender: Any?) {
73
```

```
74     }
75
76     @objc private func actionSelectArea(_ sender: Any?) {
77
78     }
79
80     @objc private func actionCaptureWindow(_ sender: Any?) {
81
82     }
83  }
```

As you may see, there are 4 menu items, but only one of them has concrete functionality, which is to exit the app (NSApp.terminate(self)). The rest of them are no-ops because of the empty action functions.

    2. Run the app. When you click on the icon, it should show a menu like the one below:

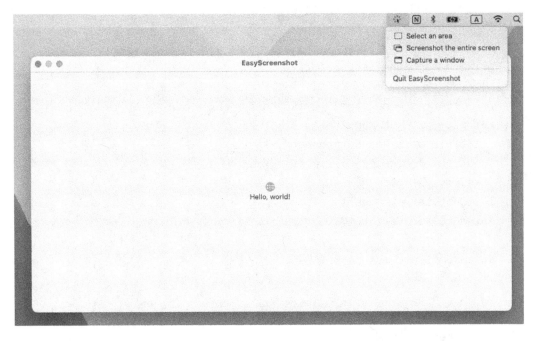

You should notice that all menu items except Quit EasyScreenshot will respond to clicks.

Removing the Main Window

You may also see a window still show up. However, we don't need it for this app.

1. Locate the `Info.plist` Values

Go to Project target -> `Building Settings` -> Filter `Info.plist`, you should be able to see a list of values under `Info.plist Values`.

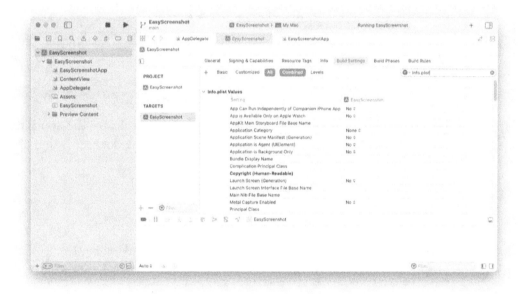

Figure 15. Info.plist Values

2. Change `Application is Agent (UIElement)` to Yes

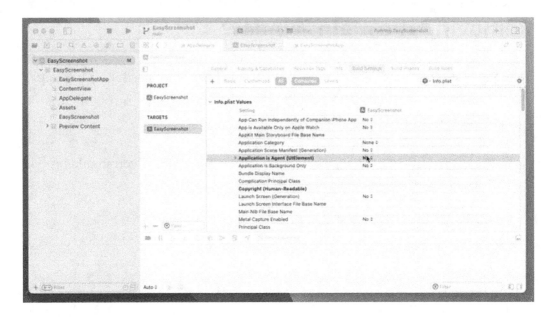

Tip What does `Application is agent(UIElement)` mean? It indicates the app is an agent app that runs in the background and doesn't appear in the dock. It is one of the key things needed to get rid of the window.

   3. Render `EmptyView()`.

Update the scene of the app by replacing it with `Settings()` and `EmptyView()`. This ensures no view is rendered for the app. `EmptyView()` represents the absence of a view.

```
1    import SwiftUI
2
3    @main
4    struct EasyScreenshotApp: App {
5      @NSApplicationDelegateAdaptor(AppDelegate.self)
6      private var appDelegate
7
8      var body: some Scene {
9        Settings {
10         EmptyView()
11       }
12     }
13   }
```

4. Run the app This is to confirm that the main window is not showing up anymore, but the menu in the status bar stays.

At this point, we should have the desired user interface for this app, however, the functionalities do not exist yet. For example, if you click on any item on the menu, nothing happens.

In the next few steps, let's fill in the functionalities.

The Screenshot App on Mac

The screenshot functionality already exists On macOS. It is an app called *Screenshot.*

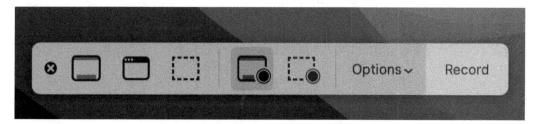

Figure 16. The Screenshot App on macOS

You can use this to screenshot the full screen, the selected window, or a selected area.

We will take advantage of this native app.

Run CLI of the Screenshot App

Now, we need to figure out how to call the Screenshot app from the Terminal:

    screencapture -h

The instructions on how to use screencapture are printed in the Terminal:

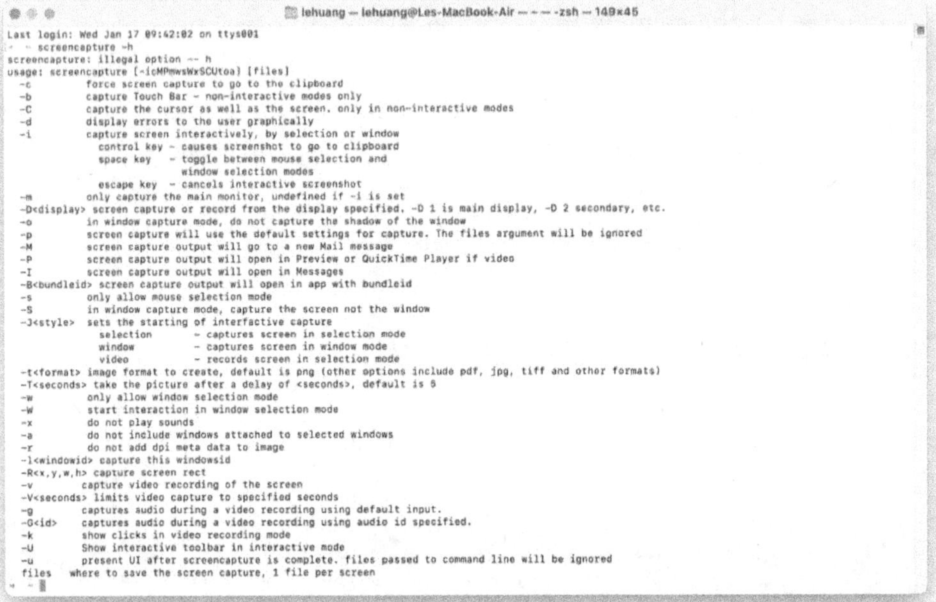

```
lehuang — lehuang@Les-MacBook-Air — ~ — -zsh — 149×45
Last login: Wed Jan 17 09:42:02 on ttys001
→  ~ screencapture -h
screencapture: illegal option -- h
usage: screencapture [-icMPmwsWxSCUtoa] [files]
  -c         force screen capture to go to the clipboard
  -b         capture Touch Bar - non-interactive modes only
  -C         capture the cursor as well as the screen. only in non-interactive modes
  -d         display errors to the user graphically
  -i         capture screen interactively, by selection or window
               control key - causes screenshot to go to clipboard
               space key   - toggle between mouse selection and
                             window selection modes
               escape key  - cancels interactive screenshot
  -m         only capture the main monitor, undefined if -i is set
  -D<display> screen capture or record from the display specified. -D 1 is main display, -D 2 secondary, etc.
  -o         in window capture mode, do not capture the shadow of the window
  -p         screen capture will use the default settings for capture. The files argument will be ignored
  -M         screen capture output will go to a new Mail message
  -P         screen capture output will open in Preview or QuickTime Player if video
  -I         screen capture output will open in Messages
  -B<bundleid> screen capture output will open in app with bundleid
  -s         only allow mouse selection mode
  -S         in window capture mode, capture the screen not the window
  -J<style>  sets the starting of interfactive capture
               selection       - captures screen in selection mode
               window          - captures screen in window mode
               video           - records screen in selection mode
  -t<format> image format to create, default is png (other options include pdf, jpg, tiff and other formats)
  -T<seconds> take the picture after a delay of <seconds>, default is 5
  -w         only allow window selection mode
  -W         start interaction in window selection mode
  -x         do not play sounds
  -a         do not include windows attached to selected windows
  -r         do not add dpi meta data to image
  -l<windowid> capture this windowsid
  -R<x,y,w,h> capture screen rect
  -v        capture video recording of the screen
  -V<seconds> limits video capture to specified seconds
  -g        captures audio during a video recording using default input.
  -G<id>    captures audio during a video recording using audio id specified.
  -k        show clicks in video recording mode
  -U        Show interactive toolbar in interactive mode
  -u        present UI after screencapture is complete. files passed to command line will be ignored
  files   where to save the screen capture, 1 file per screen
→  ~ 
```

Figure 17. The instructions of screencapture

Our requirement is to capture the screen via the following ways and store them in the *clipboard.*

1. user-selected area
2. window selection
3. fullscreen

The corresponding commands will be:

1. `screencapture -cs`
2. `screencapture -cw`
3. `screencapture -cm`

You can try the commands above and see how they behave.

Call Screenshot from App

Now, let's call these commands from the `EasyScreenshot` app.

The following snippet is how to call the command `screencapture` from an external app:

```
1   let task = Process()
2   task.launchPath = "/usr/sbin/screencapture"
3   task.arguments = ["-cw"]
4   task.launch()
5   task.waitUntilExit()
```

1. Create a utility class to handle screen capture-related actions.

Create a new file called ScreenCaptureUtil.swift and update the class with the following.

```
1   import Foundation
2
3   enum ScreenshotType {
4     case EntireScreen
5     case Window
6     case UserSelection
7   }
8
9   class ScreenCaptureUtil {
10
11    static func screenshot(type: ScreenshotType) {
12      let task = Process()
13      task.launchPath = "/usr/sbin/screencapture"
14
15      switch type {
16      case .EntireScreen:
17        task.arguments = ["-cm"]
18      case .Window:
19        task.arguments = ["-cw"]
20      case .UserSelection:
21        task.arguments = ["-cs"]
22      }
23
24      task.launch()
25      task.waitUntilExit()
26    }
27  }
```

We create a new enum to differentiate the 3 types of screenshots. When screenshot() is called, the enum variable will indicate which screenshot type is selected.

    2. Call the screenshot() when the menu item is clicked.

Now we can fill in the action functions with the respective calls to take screenshots.

```
import SwiftUI

class AppDelegate: NSObject, NSApplicationDelegate {
  ...

  @objc private func actionExitApp(_ sender: Any?) {
    NSApp.terminate(self)
  }

  @objc private func actionCaptureEntireScreen(_ sender: Any?) {
    ScreenCaptureUtil.screenshot(type: .EntireScreen)
  }

  @objc private func actionSelectArea(_ sender: Any?) {
    ScreenCaptureUtil.screenshot(type: .UserSelection)
  }

  @objc private func actionCaptureWindow(_ sender: Any?) {
    ScreenCaptureUtil.screenshot(type: .Window)
  }
}
```

    3. Run the app and try it out.

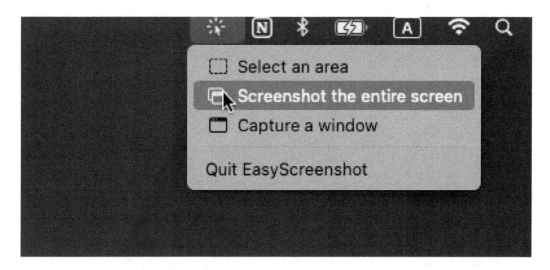

Click on one of the options in the menu. You should see a dialog like below, asking you to grant permission to record the computer screen.

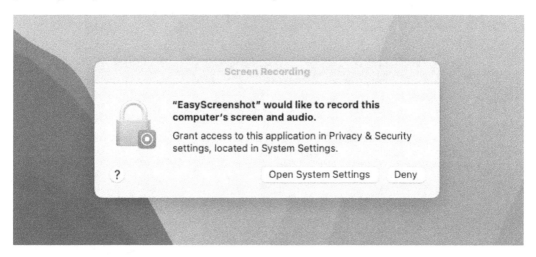

Follow the instructions to enable the recording permission for the app Simple-Screenshot. It may ask you to restart the app.

Eventually, the toggle for SimpleScreenshot should look like this:

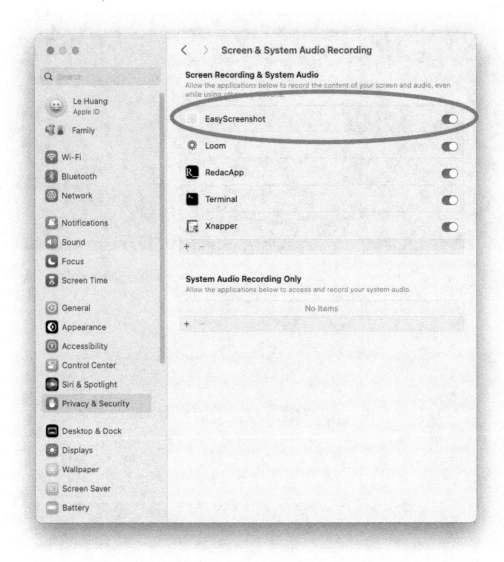

Now, you should be able to fully test the functionality of the app: click on one of the options, and it should start taking screenshots. You can view the captured image by pasting it into any editor, such as Google Docs or Microsoft Word.

You have just built another macOS app from scratch! Pretty cool, right?!

Full Code

I hope the steps are easy to follow.

In case you encounter any difficulties during the process, there's no need to worry. You can easily refer to the complete project code available at https://github.com/higracehuang/EasyScreenshot-xcode15.

If you have any questions, please feel free to reach out by sending me a note at higracehuang@gmail.com.

Potential Future Development

Here are a few features that can be added to this project:

- **Image Display**: Once the screenshot is captured in the clipboard, it will be displayed in an app window.
- **Metadata Information**: Add metadata information such as date, time, and screen resolution to the captured screenshots.
- **Screen Recording**: Expand functionality to include screen recording capabilities, allowing users to capture video along with audio.

Some of these features may require referring to additional documentation at https://developer.apple.com/xcode/swiftui/. If you are interested, give them a try.

Chapter 4: Building A Photo Fetching App

Difficulty Level: **Medium**

Besides local apps such as NumberRandomizer and EasyScreenshot that require no internet connections, in real-life applications, you may need to build an app that connects with external servers to fetch additional information. In this chapter, let's build a simple photo app that interacts with HTTP requests.

By building this app, we will become familiar with:

- Fetching HTTP requests
- Basics of SwiftUI, including ScrollView, AsyncImage

Requirements For This App

This app needs to have the following features:

- A user can fetch photos from a remote server
- A user can browse all the photos
- When a photo is clicked, a user can visit the original website

Creating A macOS App named SimplePhotos.

Choose None for Storage. We don't need Storage in this project.

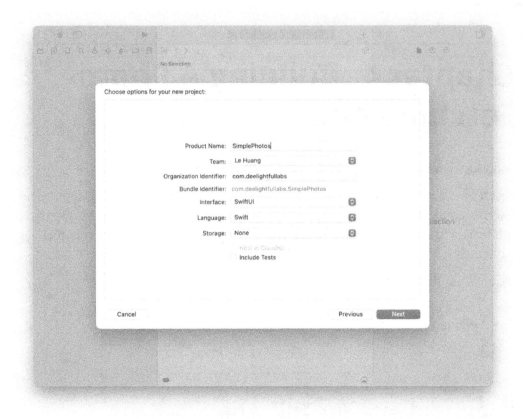

Figure 18. Create a new app without Storage

Figure 19. A new app is created

Preparing Network Calls to Fetch Photos

Before creating any user interface, let's start preparing for the network API calls. Once done, we can integrate it with the user interface.

To simplify this tutorial, we will use an existing service provided by JSONPlaceholder[1]. However, for your future projects, you may need to set up your own servers.

Here is a sample of the JSON returned from https://jsonplaceholder.typicode.com/photos:

---

[1]https://jsonplaceholder.typicode.com

```
 1  [
 2    {
 3      "albumId": 1,
 4      "id": 1,
 5      "title": "accusamus beatae ad facilis cum similique qui sunt",
 6      "url": "https://via.placeholder.com/600/92c952",
 7      "thumbnailUrl": "https://via.placeholder.com/150/92c952"
 8    },
 9    {
10      "albumId": 1,
11      "id": 2,
12      "title": "reprehenderit est deserunt velit ipsam",
13      "url": "https://via.placeholder.com/600/771796",
14      "thumbnailUrl": "https://via.placeholder.com/150/771796"
15    },
16    {
17      "albumId": 1,
18      "id": 3,
19      "title": "officia porro iure quia iusto qui ipsa ut modi",
20      "url": "https://via.placeholder.com/600/24f355",
21      "thumbnailUrl": "https://via.placeholder.com/150/24f355"
22    },
23    {
24      "albumId": 1,
25      "id": 4,
26      "title": "culpa odio esse rerum omnis laboriosam voluptate repudian\
27  dae",
28      "url": "https://via.placeholder.com/600/d32776",
29      "thumbnailUrl": "https://via.placeholder.com/150/d32776"
30    },
31    ...
32  ]
```

Above is an array of objects. Each object contains all the information about a photo.

1. Create the data model for the API response.

Create a new Swift file called `Photo.swift`. This file stores the data for one photo. The goal is to map the JSON response to a data structure in Swift, making it easily usable in the code.

```
1  import Foundation
2
3  struct Photo: Codable, Hashable {
4    let albumId: Int
5    let id: Int
6    let title: String
7    let url: String
8    let thumbnailUrl: String
9  }
```

The keys in this struct match the keys in the JSON.

2. Create a method to fetch JSON for photos.

Create a new Swift file called ApiCall.

```
1  import Foundation
2
3  class ApiCall {
4    static func getPhotos(completion: @escaping ([Photo]) -> Void) {
5      let getPhotosUrlString = "https://jsonplaceholder.typicode.com/phot\
6  os"
7
8      guard let url = URL(string: getPhotosUrlString) else { return }
9
10     URLSession.shared.dataTask(with: url) { data, response, error in
11       if let data = data,
12         let photos = try? JSONDecoder().decode([Photo].self, from: dat\
13  a) {
14         DispatchQueue.main.async {
15           completion(photos)
16         }
17       } else {
18         print("Fetch failed: \(error?.localizedDescription ?? "Unknown \
19  error")")
20       }
21     }.resume()
22   }
23  }
```

In the `getPhotos()` method, `URLSession` is used to make a network call to fetch the `Photos`. When the response returns, `JSONDecoder()` is used to parse the response into an array of Photo objects.

`URLSession` works in a background thread, although it doesn't explicitly show. So the network call to fetch photos is on a background thread, not the main thread where UI work happens.

Important to note that, it is okay to parse the JSON on a background thread, but it is a no-no to do any user interface work there.

Here, we are on a background thread processing JSON. When it is complete and the UI needs to be updated with parsed data, it should return to the main thread, by calling `DispatchQueue.main.async()`.

3. Turn on `Ongoing Connections (Client)`

By default, a macOS app cannot make network calls. This is to protect system resources and user data. To enable network connections, we need to request it through entitlements.

1. Go to **SimplePhotos(Project)**
2. Navigate to **SimplePhotos(Target)**
3. Open **Signing & Capabilities**
4. Under **App Sandbox**, turn on **Ongoing Connections (Client)**

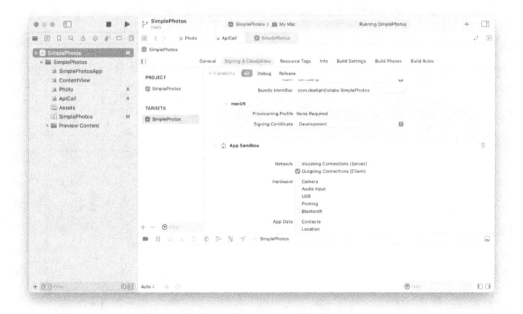

Figure 20. Turn on Ongoing Connections

The configuration above will modify the `SimplePhotos.entitlements` file.

This step is very important. If skipped, no network calls will be made. (You can try it by skipping this step and moving on to the next steps to see the difference.)

Creating User Interface

At this point, you cannot see any difference other than a blank app. In this section, we will add the user interface.

In the app, we can have a `PhotoView` to manage individual photos and a `ScrollView` to house them, as shown below:

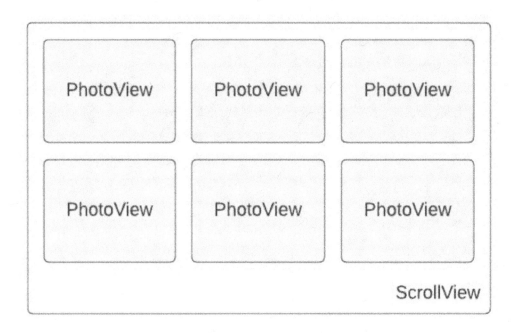

Figure 21. A ScrollView with a collection of PhotoViews

1. Create a SwiftUI `View` called `PhotoView`.

Figure 22. Create a new SwiftUI View called PhotoView

Figure 23. The code generated by SwiftUI view creation for PhotoView

2. Layout a basic view structure for PhotoView.

```
1   import SwiftUI
2
3   struct PhotoView: View {
4     var photoData: Photo
5
6     var body: some View {
7       ZStack(alignment: .bottom) {
8         AsyncImage(url: URL(string: photoData.thumbnailUrl)) { image in
9           image
10            .resizable()
11            .aspectRatio(contentMode: .fill)
12        } placeholder: {
13          Color.gray
14        }.frame(width: 200, height: 200)
15
16        Text(photoData.title)
17          .padding(5)
18          .foregroundColor(.black)
19          .frame(width: 200)
20          .lineLimit(2)
21      }
22    }
23  }
24
25  #Preview("Short title") {
26    PhotoView(photoData: Photo(
27      albumId: 1,
28      id: 1,
29      title: "short",
30      url: "https://via.placeholder.com/600/92c952",
31      thumbnailUrl: "https://via.placeholder.com/200/92c952"))
32  }
33
34  #Preview("Long title") {
35    PhotoView(photoData: Photo(
36      albumId: 1,
37      id: 1,
38      title: "officia delectus consequatur vero aut veniam",
39      url: "https://via.placeholder.com/160/56a8c2",
40      thumbnailUrl: "https://via.placeholder.com/150/56a8c2"))
```

41   }

From the code above, you may notice a few things:

- The `PhotoView` is wrapped with a `ZStack` containing `AsyncImage` in the background and `Text` in the foreground.
- `AsyncImage()` is used to display an image fetched by a network call.
- The fetched image is resized to fill the frame of 200 x 200.
- When the image is not received, it shows a placeholder with a gray background.
- The title of the photo is displayed in black with a limit of 2 lines.
- Two previews are added so we can compare how the view looks with different lengths of content.

Figure 24. Preview of PhotoView on the right pane

3. In `ContentView.swift`, create a `ScrollView` to contain all `PhotoViews`.

Now, let's update the `ContentView` to display the photos.

```
1   import SwiftUI
2
3   struct ContentView: View {
4     @State var photos:[Photo] = []
5
6     let columns = [GridItem](repeating: GridItem(.flexible()), count: 4)
7
8     var body: some View {
9       ScrollView {
10        LazyVGrid(columns: columns) {
11          ForEach(photos, id: \.self) { photo in
12            PhotoView(photoData: photo)
13          }
14        }
15        .padding(.horizontal)
16        .onAppear {
17          ApiCall.getPhotos(completion: { photos in
18            self.photos = photos
19          })
20        }.padding()
21      }.frame(minWidth: 900, minHeight: 800)
22    }
23  }
24
25  #Preview {
26      ContentView()
27  }
```

From the code above, you may notice a few things:

- Introduce a @State variable called photos to store the result of the
  ApiCall.getPhotos().
- Define a ScrollView with a 4-column LazyVGrid.
- Inside the LazyVGrid, display all the PhotoViews.
- When the view appears, make a call to ApiCall.getPhotos() to fetch all
  photos, implicitly in the background thread.
- Set the overall size of the app window to 900 x 800.

Tip LazyVGrid is a container view that arranges its child views in a grid that grows vertically, creating items only when they need to be displayed. On the contrary, a Grid view creates its child views right away.

A "sister" of LazyVGrid is LazyHGrid. LazyHGrid arranges its child views in a grid that grows horizontally.

Tip ScrollView is a scrollable container view where you can display content. This view automatically adjusts its size to fit the content inside. ScrollView can be scrolled horizontally, vertically, or both.

Figure 25. The preview of ContentView

Tada! 🎉 This app is getting together, right? We can make more UI tweaks.

4. Update PhotoView to only show text on mouseover.

```
1   import SwiftUI
2
3   struct PhotoView: View {
4     var photoData: Photo
5
6     @State private var isOver = false
7
8     var body: some View {
9       ZStack(alignment: .bottom) {
10        AsyncImage(url: URL(string: photoData.thumbnailUrl)) { image in
11          image
12            .resizable()
13            .aspectRatio(contentMode: .fill)
14        } placeholder: {
15          Color.gray
16        }.frame(width: 200, height: 200)
17
18        if isOver {
19          Text(photoData.title)
20            .padding(5)
21            .foregroundColor(.black)
22            .frame(width: 200)
23            .lineLimit(2)
24        }
25      }.onHover { isOver in
26        self.isOver = isOver
27      }
28    }
29  }
30
31  #Preview("Short title") {
32    PhotoView(photoData: Photo(
33      albumId: 1,
34      id: 1,
35      title: "short",
36      url: "https://via.placeholder.com/600/92c952",
37      thumbnailUrl: "https://via.placeholder.com/200/92c952"))
38  }
39
40  #Preview("Long title") {
```

```
41    PhotoView(photoData: Photo(
42      albumId: 1,
43      id: 1,
44      title: "officia delectus consequatur vero aut veniam",
45      url: "https://via.placeholder.com/160/56a8c2",
46      thumbnailUrl: "https://via.placeholder.com/150/56a8c2"))
47  }
```

You may notice some tweaks from the original PhotoView:

- Add a @State variable called isOver.
- Update the variable isOver when the mouse hovers over the ZStack.
- Show the title if isOver is true. Otherwise, don't render the title.

When you run the app, you can verify the hover behavior.

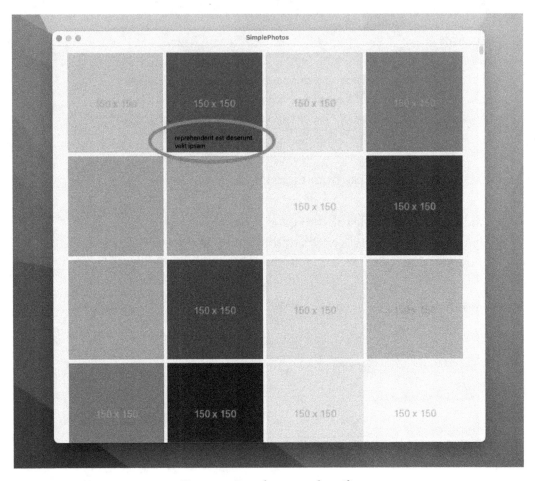

Figure 26. Run the app and verify

5. Implement the click behavior: when the photo is clicked, it opens a URL.

```
1   import SwiftUI
2
3   struct PhotoView: View {
4     var photoData: Photo
5
6     @State private var isOver = false
7
8     var body: some View {
9       Link(destination: URL(string: photoData.url)!) {
10        ZStack(alignment: .bottom) {
11          AsyncImage(url: URL(string: photoData.thumbnailUrl)) { image in
```

```
12        image
13           .resizable()
14           .aspectRatio(contentMode: .fill)
15        } placeholder: {
16           Color.gray
17        }.frame(width: 200, height: 200)
18
19        if isOver {
20           Text(photoData.title)
21              .padding(5)
22              .foregroundColor(.black)
23              .frame(width: 200)
24              .lineLimit(2)
25        }
26     }.onHover { isOver in
27        self.isOver = isOver
28     }
29   }
30  }
31 }
32
33 #Preview("Short title") {
34   PhotoView(photoData: Photo(
35     albumId: 1,
36     id: 1,
37     title: "short",
38     url: "https://via.placeholder.com/600/92c952",
39     thumbnailUrl: "https://via.placeholder.com/200/92c952"))
40  }
41
42 #Preview("Long title") {
43   PhotoView(photoData: Photo(
44     albumId: 1,
45     id: 1,
46     title: "officia delectus consequatur vero aut veniam",
47     url: "https://via.placeholder.com/160/56a8c2",
48     thumbnailUrl: "https://via.placeholder.com/150/56a8c2"))
49  }
```

To make the photo clickable, `Link()` now wraps the original `ZStack`.

When you run the app and click any photo in the app, it should immediately open a new URL in Safari.

That's it! A pretty basic photo viewer is complete.

6. Run the app, and scroll through the photos.

You can see the photos are lazy loaded into the app. To verify the network calls are indeed triggered on demand, open the debug navigator, and click the Network tab.

As you scroll through, you can see the network receiving and sending rates being positive.

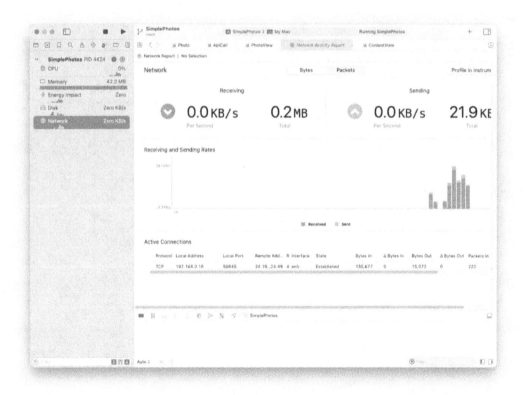

Figure 27. Receiving and Sending Rates are positive when you scroll through the photos in the app

Tip Debug Navigator is a very effective way to help evaluate the performance of your app.

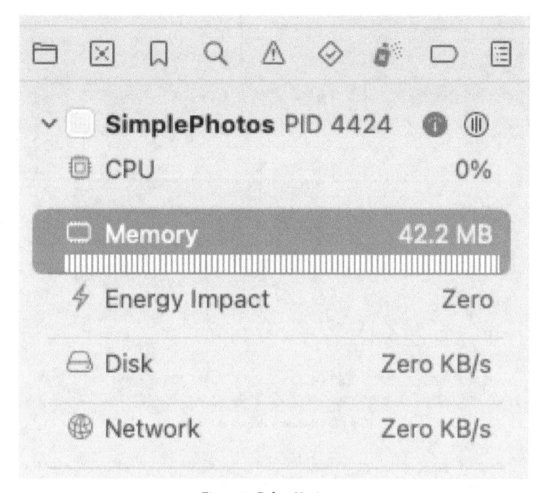

Figure 28. Debug Navigator

When your app is running in Xcode, you can check the Memory tab. It shows the current memory usage. If the usage is too high, it may trigger a warning. The app would risk termination if the memory usage enters the red area.

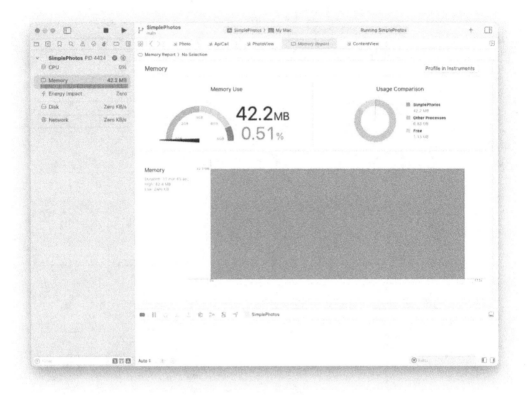

Figure 29. Memory Report of the app

When your app appears to have high memory usage, consider checking whether the following are the root causes, and fix or optimize them accordingly:

- **Memory leaks**: Investigate and address any memory leaks in your code.
- **Heavy animations**: Optimize or reduce the complexity of animations that might be consuming a significant amount of memory.
- **Image assets are too large**: Resize or compress large image assets to reduce their memory footprint.
- **The size of Core Data transactions is too big**: Break down large Core Data transactions into smaller, more manageable portions.
- **Unused views being used**: Ensure that unused views are not retained in memory and consider implementing proper view lifecycle management.

Congratulations! One more macOS app is under your belt!

Full Code

You can find the code on Github https://github.com/higracehuang/SimplePhotos-xcode15.

If you have any questions, please feel free to reach out by sending me a note at higracehuang@gmail.com.

Potential Future Development

Here are a few features that can be added to this project:

- **Image Display**: Allow users to view the image in a separate window after clicking on it in the scroll view.
- **Error Handling**: Implement a robust error handling mechanism to gracefully handle scenarios where image loading fails or there is no internet connection.
- **Image Sharing**: Enable users to share images with others via email, messaging apps, or social media directly from the app.

If any of these piques your interest, give it a try. If not, feel free to move on to the next chapter.

Chapter 5: Building A Note-taking App

Difficulty Level: **Hard**

All the apps we've built so far have required very simple data models, but what if you need to manage complex data models, such as those in MySQL databases? You can also do that in macOS development using Core Data.

In this chapter, we will build a very simple note-taking app that involves storing data models:

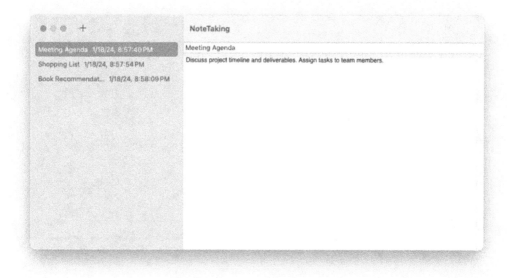

Figure 30. Note-taking App

By building this, we will get familiar with:

- The process to create a macOS app in general
- How to use Core Data for local storage
- Basics of SwiftUI

71

Requirements For This App

This note-taking app needs to have the following features:

- A user can view all the notes.
- A user can create, edit, and delete any note.
- The note persists after the app quits.
- Each note should have the following fields: title, content, creation timestamp, and update timestamp.

Creating A macOS App named NoteTaking.

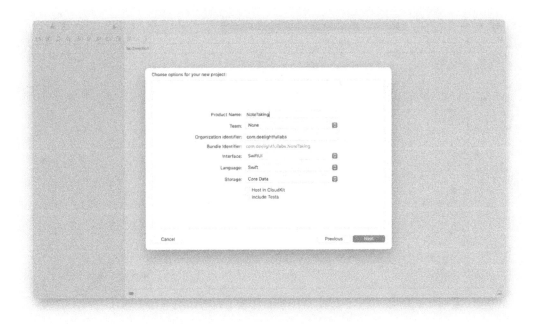

Figure 31. App Information

When setting up the app, choose Core Data as the storage option. Core Data will be used for managing data structure, relationships, and storage in this project.

Tip: Core Data is a framework for managing data object graphs in applications, commonly used for local data storage.

In our note-taking app, we'll need to store notes on the device, and we'll explore Core Data further in the upcoming sections.

If you're unsure whether your app will use Core Data, you have the option not to enable it initially. You can set it up later if needed.

After the project is created, Xcode generates the code for a basic macOS app with the necessary boilerplates and begins building the project upon creation.

As you can see in the snapshot above:

- On the left pane, it shows the file structure of the project.

    - NoteTakingApp: This Swift file represents the main structure of your Xcode project. It contains the primary code and configurations for your app.
    - ContentView: This file typically contains the main SwiftUI view of your app. It defines the structure and layout of the user interface.
    - Assets: This is where you can store and organize any image assets or media files used in your app.
    - Persistnence: This Swift file likely contains code related to data persistence or storage. It plays a role in managing how your app's data is stored or retrieved.
    - NoteTaking Entitlements: This file may include entitlements for your app, specifying permissions and capabilities it has on the device.
    - NoteTaking Core Data (NoteTaking.xcdatamodeld): This folder likely contains files and configurations related to Core Data, which is a framework used for data storage and management in your app.

- On the right pane, it is the preview of the app, where Xcode offers a live representation of the user interface, allowing developers to visualize and interact with design changes in real-time.
- The middle pane shows the generated code, with `ContentView` shown.

At this point, the code we have so far is also committed to your local git history.

Playing With the App

Now we have a working starter app! Let's try it.

1. Click the ▶ button on the left pane of Xcode, to run the app.

Once the build is complete, you will see a functioning app, like this:

Figure 32. A functioning starter app

In this app, you can see:

- A + sign on the top
- A left pane
- A right pane

2. Click the + sign, and an entry will be created on the left pane.

When you click on the new entry, the right pane will be updated with new content.

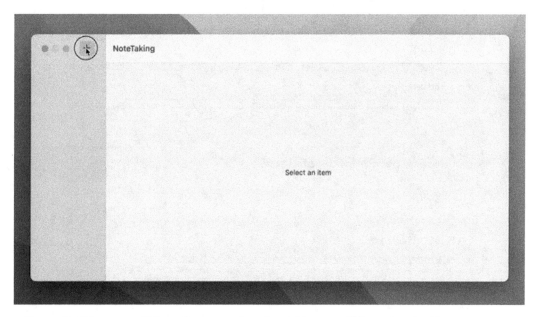

Figure 33. When you click on the new entry, the right pane will be updated with new content.

It's pretty cool, right? With this, we can easily add more features to the existing code. Let's go!

Diving Deep into ContentView code

In Xcode, click to open ContentView.swift.

```
1   import SwiftUI
2   import CoreData
3
4   struct ContentView: View {
5     @Environment(\.managedObjectContext) private var viewContext
6
7     @FetchRequest(
8       sortDescriptors: [NSSortDescriptor(keyPath: \Item.timestamp, ascend\
9   ing: true)],
10      animation: .default)
11    private var items: FetchedResults<Item>
```

```
12
13    var body: some View {
14      NavigationView {
15        List {
16          ForEach(items) { item in
17            NavigationLink {
18              Text("Item at \(item.timestamp!, formatter: itemFormatter)")
19            } label: {
20              Text(item.timestamp!, formatter: itemFormatter)
21            }
22          }
23          .onDelete(perform: deleteItems)
24        }
25        .toolbar {
26          ToolbarItem {
27            Button(action: addItem) {
28              Label("Add Item", systemImage: "plus")
29            }
30          }
31        }
32        Text("Select an item")
33      }
34    }
35
36    private func addItem() {
37      withAnimation {
38        let newItem = Item(context: viewContext)
39        newItem.timestamp = Date()
40
41        do {
42          try viewContext.save()
43        } catch {
44          let nsError = error as NSError
45          fatalError("Unresolved error \(nsError), \(nsError.userInfo)")
46        }
47      }
48    }
49
50    private func deleteItems(offsets: IndexSet) {
51      withAnimation {
```

```
52        offsets.map { items[$0] }.forEach(viewContext.delete)
53
54        do {
55          try viewContext.save()
56        } catch {
57          let nsError = error as NSError
58          fatalError("Unresolved error \(nsError), \(nsError.userInfo)")
59        }
60      }
61    }
62  }
63
64  private let itemFormatter: DateFormatter = {
65    let formatter = DateFormatter()
66    formatter.dateStyle = .short
67    formatter.timeStyle = .medium
68    return formatter
69  }()
70
71  #Preview {
72    ContentView().environment(\.managedObjectContext, PersistenceControll\
73  er.preview.container.viewContext)
74  }
```

Let's break it down and take a look at how it works.

Preview

In this file, you can see two structs: `ContentView` and `Preview`.

```
1  struct ContentView: View {
2      ...
3  }
```

The `ContentView` struct describes the content and layout that the app will rely on.

```
1   #Preview {
2       ContentView().environment(\.managedObjectContext, PersistenceContro\
3   ller.preview.container.viewContext)
4   }
```

The `Preview` struct describes how to show the preview (a.k.a., canvas) on the right pane for `ContentView`. It is very helpful during development: whenever the view is updated, without running the app, you can easily see what it looks like in the Preview.

Here are a few things about the Preview:

- When the app is running, it does not execute the `Preview` at all.
- If you prefer not to use the preview, you can simply remove the `Preview` struct.
- You can have multiple previews for one view.

Environment Variable

```
1   @Environment(\.managedObjectContext) private var viewContext
```

`managedObjectContext` is used here to facilitate *saving* and *deleting* Core Data. However, fetching Core Data does not need `managedObjectContext`.

In this view, `manageObjectContext` is passed as an environment variable. But where does it get passed?

It is defined in `Persistence`, and then referenced in `NoteTakingApp`, and eventually read in `ContentView` by adding an `@Environment` property.

```
1   struct PersistenceController {
2       static let shared = PersistenceController()
3
4       ...
5
6       let container: NSPersistentContainer
7
8       ...
9   }
```

```
1   import SwiftUI
2
3   @main
4   struct NoteTakingApp: App {
5       let persistenceController = PersistenceController.shared
6
7       var body: some Scene {
8           WindowGroup {
9               ContentView()
10                      .environment(\.managedObjectContext, persistenceControl\
11  ler.container.viewContext)
12          }
13      }
14  }
```

@Environment is one way to manage shared resources in SwiftUI. We will discuss this as well as other alternatives in Chapter 5.

FetchRequest

```
1   @FetchRequest(
2       sortDescriptors: [NSSortDescriptor(keyPath: \Item.timestamp, ascend\
3   ing: true)],
4       animation: .default)
5   private var items: FetchedResults<Item>
```

When ContentView is created, it will fetch a collection of items from the Core Data persistence store. The results will be sorted by the ascending timestamp.

NavigationView

```
1   var body: some View {
2       NavigationView {
3           List {
4               ForEach(items) { item in
5                   NavigationLink {
6                       ...
7                   }
8               }
9               .onDelete(perform: deleteItems)
10          }
11          ...
12      }
13  }
```

The foundation of the ContentView is this NavigationView. NavigationView is a user interface where the user clicks on a NavigationLink on one pane, and the destination of the NavigationLink will display on the other pane.

Inside the NavigationView, a List hosts a collection of NavigationLinks.

Adding and Deleting Items

Two functions handle the data transactions: addItem() and deleteItems().

```
1   private func addItem() {
2       withAnimation {
3           let newItem = Item(context: viewContext)
4           newItem.timestamp = Date()
5           do {
6               try viewContext.save()
7           } catch {
8               let nsError = error as NSError
9               fatalError("Unresolved error \(nsError), \(nsError.userInfo\
10  )")
11          }
12      }
13  }
```

Item is an entity in Core Data. Item() creates an entry of the entity Item, and will be saved to Core Data. This happens when addItem is called.

```
1  private func deleteItems(offsets: IndexSet) {
2      withAnimation {
3          offsets.map { items[$0] }.forEach(viewContext.delete)
4
5          do {
6              try viewContext.save()
7          } catch {
8              let nsError = error as NSError
9              fatalError("Unresolved error \(nsError), \(nsError.userInfo\
10 )")
11         }
12     }
13 }
```

Similarly, given a set of indexes of items, deleteItems() deletes them from the Core Data.

Date Formatter

```
1  private let itemFormatter: DateFormatter = {
2      let formatter = DateFormatter()
3      formatter.dateStyle = .short
4      formatter.timeStyle = .medium
5      return formatter
6  }()
```

The itemFormatter defines how timestamp is being formatted.

In the code, the date format is defined as short, so an example of the output is 3/28/17 - mm/dd/yy.

The time format is defined as medium, so an example of the output is 1:26:32 PM.

For both time and date, they are other types of formats. You can change to fit your needs, according to the Apple Developer Documentation[1].

Designing the Data Model

At this point, we know how the generated code works. We can make changes on top of it to make this app into a note-taking app.

---

[1]https://developer.apple.com/documentation/foundation/dateformatter

Current Data Model

In the Project Navigator, click the `NoteTaking.xcdatamodeld`.

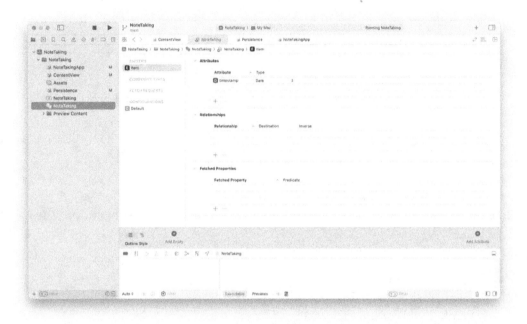

Figure 34. NoteTaking.xcdatamodeld

Currently, it only has one entity called `Item`, and the entity Item has one attribute called `timestamp`.

Requirements for the Data Model

As described in the beginning, for the note-taking app, for each note entry, we will need the following:

- **Title**: String, Required
- **Content**: String, Optional
- **Creation timestamp**: Date, Required
- **Update timestamp**: Date, Required

Let's configure the Core Data.

Adding a New Entity

We will create a brand new entity for our use case, instead of using the original entity Item.

1. Click Add Entity. A new entity called Entity will be created.
2. Double click the entity Entity, to rename Entity To NoteEntry.
3. Under Attributes, click + to add the following:

   - content as String
   - title as String
   - createdAt as Date
   - updatedAt as Date

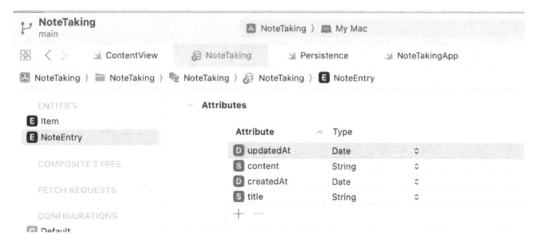

Figure 35. Adding all attributes in Core Data

4. For the attributes title and createdAt, use the data model inspector (choose View > Inspectors > Show Data Model Inspector) to configure them to be not Optional.

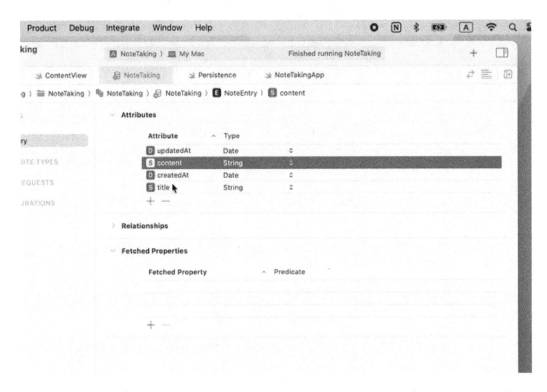

Setting the attributes `title` and `createdAt` to be not `Optional` in the data model means that every note entry must have a title and a creation timestamp.

5. Run the app.

The build should be successful because we haven't added anything to the code logic yet.

Tip: Running the app after adding a new entity in Core Data is important to ensure that the data model changes are reflected in the app and the underlying SQLite database. When you add a new entity or make modifications to the data model, it doesn't automatically apply those changes to the existing database.

Reading Core Data from `ContentView`

Creating a `FetchRequest` for `NoteEntry`

1. Similar to the Item `FetchedRequest`, create another for `NoteEntry`. In addition, we want to sort the entries by the creation timestamp.

```
1   @FetchRequest(
2   sortDescriptors: [NSSortDescriptor(keyPath: \NoteEntry.createdAt, ascen\
3   ding: true)], animation: .default)
4   private var noteEntries: FetchedResults<NoteEntry>
5
```

2. Run the app now.

It should have no errors. The user interface should still look like it was before. The app is pulling note entries from Core Data, but it has no record yet.

Displaying NoteEntry

Now, we can read and display the note entries from the FetchRequest that we just did.

1. Replace the body of ContentView with the following:

```
1    var body: some View {
2      NavigationView {
3        List {
4          ForEach(noteEntries) { noteEntry in
5            if let title = noteEntry.title,
6               let content = noteEntry.content,
7               let updatedAt = noteEntry.updatedAt {
8              NavigationLink {
9                Text(content)
10             } label: {
11               Text(title)
12               Text(updatedAt, formatter: itemFormatter)
13             }
14           }
15         }
16         .onDelete(perform: deleteItems)
17       }
18       .toolbar {
19         ToolbarItem {
20           Button(action: addItem) {
```

```
21              Label("Add Note", systemImage: "plus")
22            }
23          }
24        }
25      Text("Select a note")
26    }
27  }
```

Instead of reading the old Item entity, now we are reading the entity NoteEntry entity that we've just created.

Notice the if and let statement wraps around NavigationLink? Let me explain.

The attributes of an entity are optional by default. Even though some of them are defined as non-optional in Core Data, the generated attributes are still optional in Swift language.

Therefore, when we want to display the attributes in views, we need to unwrap the optional and get the value.

We have 3 options to unwrap the optionals: optional binding, unconditional unwrapping, and using the nil-coalescing operator.

Optional Binding

```
1   if let title = noteEntry.title,
2      let content = noteEntry.content,
3      let updatedAt = noteEntry.updatedAt {
4      NavigationLink {
5        Text(content)
6      } label: {
7        Text(title)
8        Text(updatedAt, formatter: itemFormatter)
9      }
10  }
```

Unconditional Unwrapping

```
1  ForEach(noteEntries) { noteEntry in
2    NavigationLink {
3      Text(noteEntry.content!)
4    } label: {
5      Text(noteEntry.title!)
6      Text(noteEntry.updatedAt!, formatter: itemFormatter)
7    }
8  }
```

If you are sure that the attribute is never nil, you can simply use the forced unwrap operator (postfix !) to get the value directly. Be cautious when using the forced unwrap operator. If it happens to be nil, the app may crash.

Using the nil-coalescing operator

```
1  NavigationLink {
2    Text(noteEntry.content ?? "")
3  } label: {
4    Text(noteEntry.title ?? "Untitled")
5    Text(noteEntry.updatedAt ?? Date(), formatter: itemFormatter)
6  }
```

Use the nil-coalescing operator (??) to supply a default value in case the Optional instance is nil.

Optional Binding is my favorite of all at most times. It is safe and structured easily. You can choose the option that fits your use case.

Read more about Optional at Apple Developer Documentation[2].

Tip: A quick way to format your code properly is to format the code and press Control + I. It is very handy when you need to change a lot of code all of sudden. You don't have to worry about the correct indentation at the time of change. You will only need to format afterward.

Adding New Entry to NoteEntry Entity

We now update the addItem function to update NoteEntries, instead of Items.

1. Rename all of the occurrences of addItem to addNoteEntry.

---

[2]https://developer.apple.com/documentation/swift/optional

To do it, you can highlight any of the `addItem` occurrences, right-click to see the menu, and choose `Refactor -> Rename....`

```
▶  ⎇ NoteTaking                    🅰 NoteTaking ) 🖥 My Mac              Build Succeeded | To
      main

 ⊞  ⊟  ⊞  ⟨ ⟩  🔗 ContentView     🅰 NoteTaking     🔗 NoteTaking     🔗 Persistence      🔗 NoteTak

🅰 NoteTaking ) 📁 NoteTaking ) 🔗 ContentView ) 🔲 body

   4   struct ContentView: View {
  18     var body: some View {
  24              let updatedAt = noteEntry.updatedAt {
  25            NavigationLink {
  26              Text(content)
  27            } label: {
  28              Text(title)          Jump to Definition
  29              Text(updatedAt,      Show Callers...
  30            }
  31          }                        Show Quick Help
  32        }                          Edit All in Scope
  33        .onDelete(perform: de      Create Code Snippet...
  34      }
  35      .toolbar {                   Show SwiftUI Inspector...
  36        ToolbarItem {
  37          Button(action: addI      Extract Subview
  38            Label("Add Note",      Embed in HStack
  39          }                        Embed in VStack
  40        }                          Embed in ZStack
  41      }                            Embed in List
  42      Text("Select a note")        Group
  43    }                              Make Conditional
  44  }                                Repeat
  45                                   Embed...
  46
  47    private func addItem() {       Embed...
  48      withAnimation {
  49        let newItem = Item(cont    Refactor          ⟩
  50        newItem.timestamp = Dat    Find              ⟩
  51                                   Navigate          ⟩
  52        do {
  53          try viewContext.save(    Fold
  54        } catch {
  55          // Replace this imple    Show Last Change for Line
```

2. Update the function `addNoteEntry` to create new `NoteEntry`.

```
1   private func addNoteEntry() {
2     withAnimation {
3       let newNoteEntry = NoteEntry(context: viewContext)
4
5       newNoteEntry.createdAt = Date()
6       newNoteEntry.updatedAt = Date()
7       newNoteEntry.title = "Untitled"
8       newNoteEntry.content = "TBD"
9
10      do {
11        try viewContext.save()
12      } catch {
13        let nsError = error as NSError
14        fatalError("Unresolved error \(nsError), \(nsError.userInfo)")
15      }
16    }
17  }
```

Initial values are set for the new note entry, including timestamps (createdAt and updatedAt), temporary dummy data for the title ("Untitled"), and content ("TBD").

3. Run the app.

Click the + button, it should create a note entry. Click on the title of the new entry, it should display TBD as expected.

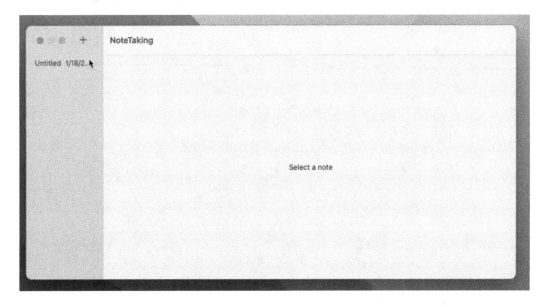

Wonderful progress! We now can confirm the app is reading the NoteEntries entity we just created.

Updating Note Entries

We want to have our values for note title and note content, rather than constant values like Untitled and TBD.

Refactor the transaction functions

Before we start to change the view, let's clean up the code and do some preparation.

1. Move addNoteEntry() from ContentView to Persistence, as one of the members in PersistenceController.

Because viewContext will be missing in the Persistence, we also add:

```
1   let viewContext = container.viewContext.
```

The Persistence will look like this after the change:

```
1    import CoreData
2
3    struct PersistenceController {
4      static let shared = PersistenceController()
5
6      static var preview: PersistenceController = {
7        let result = PersistenceController(inMemory: true)
8        let viewContext = result.container.viewContext
9        for _ in 0..<10 {
10         let newItem = Item(context: viewContext)
11         newItem.timestamp = Date()
12       }
13       do {
14         try viewContext.save()
15       } catch {
16         let nsError = error as NSError
```

```
17        fatalError("Unresolved error \(nsError), \(nsError.userInfo)")
18      }
19    return result
20  }()
21
22  let container: NSPersistentContainer
23
24  init(inMemory: Bool = false) {
25    container = NSPersistentContainer(name: "NoteTaking")
26    if inMemory {
27      container.persistentStoreDescriptions.first!.url = URL(fileURLWit\
28 hPath: "/dev/null")
29    }
30    container.loadPersistentStores(completionHandler: { (storeDescripti\
31 on, error) in
32      if let error = error as NSError? {
33        fatalError("Unresolved error \(error), \(error.userInfo)")
34      }
35    })
36    container.viewContext.automaticallyMergesChangesFromParent = true
37  }
38
39  func addNoteEntry() {
40    let viewContext = container.viewContext
41    let newNoteEntry = NoteEntry(context: viewContext)
42    newNoteEntry.createdAt = Date()
43    newNoteEntry.updatedAt = Date()
44    newNoteEntry.title = "Untitled"
45    newNoteEntry.content = "TBD"
46
47    do {
48      try viewContext.save()
49    } catch {
50      let nsError = error as NSError
51      fatalError("Unresolved error \(nsError), \(nsError.userInfo)")
52    }
53  }
54 }
```

This way, we can keep transactional code in one place.

2. In `ContentView`, Update the callers of the `addNoteEntry` function accordingly.

```
1  ToolbarItem {
2    Button(action: PersistenceController.shared.addNoteEntry) {
3      Label("Add Note", systemImage: "plus")
4    }
5  }
```

3. In `ContentView`, delete `deleteItems()` and its reference.

At this moment, we don't need the functionality.

Delete the function definition:

```
1  private func deleteItems(offsets: IndexSet) {
2    withAnimation {
3      offsets.map { items[$0] }.forEach(viewContext.delete)
4
5      do {
6        try viewContext.save()
7      } catch {
8        // Replace this implementation with code to handle the error appr\
9  opriately.
10        // fatalError() causes the application to generate a crash log an\
11  d terminate. You should not use this function in a shipping application
12  , although it may be useful during development.
13        let nsError = error as NSError
14        fatalError("Unresolved error \(nsError), \(nsError.userInfo)")
15      }
16    }
17  }
```

Delete the reference:

```
1  .onDelete(perform: deleteItems)
```

4. In `ContentView`, delete the `FetchRequest` for `Item`.

We don't use the entity Item anymore. We only use `NoteEntry`.

Delete the following from the code.

```
1  @FetchRequest(
2    sortDescriptors: [NSSortDescriptor(keyPath: \Item.timestamp, ascendin\
3  g: true)],
4    animation: .default)
5  private var items: FetchedResults<Item>
```

After the code cleanup, the ContentView is a lot cleaner and should look like this:

```
1   import SwiftUI
2   import CoreData
3
4   struct ContentView: View {
5     @Environment(\.managedObjectContext) private var viewContext
6
7     @FetchRequest(
8       sortDescriptors: [NSSortDescriptor(keyPath: \NoteEntry.createdAt, a\
9   scending: true)], animation: .default)
10    private var noteEntries: FetchedResults<NoteEntry>
11
12
13    var body: some View {
14      NavigationView {
15        List {
16          ForEach(noteEntries) { noteEntry in
17            if let title = noteEntry.title,
18               let content = noteEntry.content,
19               let updatedAt = noteEntry.updatedAt {
20              NavigationLink {
21                Text(content)
22              } label: {
23                Text(title)
24                Text(updatedAt, formatter: itemFormatter)
25              }
26            }
27          }
28        }
29        .toolbar {
30          ToolbarItem {
31            Button(action: PersistenceController.shared.addNoteEntry) {
32              Label("Add Note", systemImage: "plus")
```

```
33              }
34            }
35          }
36        Text("Select a note")
37      }
38    }
39 }
40
41 private let itemFormatter: DateFormatter = {
42    let formatter = DateFormatter()
43    formatter.dateStyle = .short
44    formatter.timeStyle = .medium
45    return formatter
46 }()
47
48 #Preview {
49    ContentView().environment(\.managedObjectContext, PersistenceControll\
50 er.preview.container.viewContext)
51 }
```

This lays out a good foundation for the next step.

    5. Run the app to verify everything is functional as before.

Adding Text Inputs

At this moment, both the title and content are temporary dummy data. We can make them dynamic. Let's add form elements to the app: an input for the title and an input for the content.

Wait, it is not that simple! If we have 100 note entries, should there be 100 title inputs and 100 content inputs? How can we manage them in the code?

We need to modularize the code in ContentView even more to easily manage this. Let's make each note entry its own View: NoteEntryView!

    1. Create a new View in ContentView.swift called NoteEntryView.

```
1   struct NoteEntryView: View {
2     var noteEntry: NoteEntry
3
4     var body: some View {
5       if let title = noteEntry.title,
6          let content = noteEntry.content,
7          let updatedAt = noteEntry.updatedAt {
8         NavigationLink {
9           Text(content)
10        } label: {
11          Text(title)
12          Text(updatedAt, formatter: itemFormatter)
13        }
14      }
15    }
16  }
```

2. Use `NoteEntryView` in `ContentView`

```
1   var body: some View {
2     NavigationView {
3       List {
4         ForEach(noteEntries) { noteEntry in
5           NoteEntryView(noteEntry: noteEntry) //<<<<
6         }
7       }
8       .toolbar {
9         ToolbarItem {
10          Button(action: PersistenceController.shared.addNoteEntry) {
11            Label("Add Note", systemImage: "plus")
12          }
13        }
14      }
15      Text("Select a note")
16    }
17  }
```

3. Add text inputs to `NoteEntryView`.

Update the view `NoteEntryView` with the following:

```
1    struct NoteEntryView: View {
2      var noteEntry: NoteEntry
3
4      @State private var titleInput: String = ""
5      @State private var contentInput: String = ""
6
7      var body: some View {
8        if let title = noteEntry.title,
9           let content = noteEntry.content,
10          let updatedAt = noteEntry.updatedAt {
11         NavigationLink {
12           VStack {
13             TextField("Title", text: $titleInput)
14               .onAppear() {
15                 self.titleInput = title
16               }
17             TextEditor(text: $contentInput)
18               .onAppear() {
19                 self.contentInput = content
20               }
21           }
22         } label: {
23           Text(title)
24           Text(updatedAt, formatter: itemFormatter)
25         }
26        }
27      }
28    }
```

You may notice a few changes here:

- Replace Text() with TextField() and TextEditor(). Text() displays plain text that users cannot update. TextField() and TextEditor() are inputs that users can engage with.
- Add two @State variables to store the values of the two inputs
- When the inputs are being displayed, i.e. onAppear(), assign the noteEntry information fetched from Core Data to the input values.

4. Run the app and verify the changes.

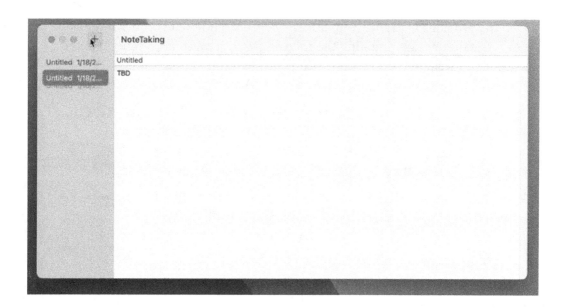

Adding Update Function

Similarly to the operations of adding note entries, we need to add a function to handle the transaction: saving the user-specified values for the title and the content to Core Data.

1. Add the method updateNoteEntry() to the Persistence.swift, to be next to other transactional methods such as addNoteEntry().

```
func updateNoteEntry(noteEntry: NoteEntry, title:String, content: Strin\
g) {
  let viewContext = container.viewContext
  noteEntry.content = content
  noteEntry.title = title
  noteEntry.updatedAt = Date()

  do {
    try viewContext.save()
  } catch {
    let nsError = error as NSError
    fatalError("Unresolved error \(nsError), \(nsError.userInfo)")
  }
}
```

Given the provided noteEntry, update the content and the title with the new values. Because we are updating the note entry, so we also need to update the updatedAt as well.

Calling Update Function When Inputs Are Changed

The input views TextField() and TextEditor() have the same method onChange(). This method is triggered when the input value is changed.

We need to call the update function when onChange() is called, so here we continue to chain onChange() to the inputs in the code.

1. In NoteEntryView, add onChange() for the titleInput.

```
1   TextField("Title", text: $titleInput)
2       .onAppear() {
3           self.titleInput = title
4       }
5       .onChange(of: titleInput) { oldTitle, newTitle in
6           PersistenceController.shared.updateNoteEntry(
7           noteEntry: noteEntry, title: newTitle, content: contentInput)
8       }
```

2. In NoteEntryView, add onChange() for the contentInput.

```
1   TextEditor(text: $contentInput)
2       .onAppear() {
3           self.contentInput = content
4       }
5       .onChange(of: contentInput) { oldContent, newContent in
6           PersistenceController.shared.updateNoteEntry(
7           noteEntry: noteEntry, title: titleInput, content: newContent)
8       }
```

3. In NoteEntryView, change the variable noteEntry to be @ObservedObject.

```
1  @ObservedObject var noteEntry: NoteEntry
```

Note that, This step is very important for keeping the views updated.

The variable `noteEntry` is passed from the parent `ContentView`. With the type `@ObservedObject`, whenever `noteEntry` is changed, the `NoteEntryView` will be invalidated and redrawn. Read more about `@ObservedObject` in Chapter 5.

(You can also experiment by skipping this step and see how the app behaves differently. You may notice the inputs not displayed consistently.)

With the above changes, here is what `ContentView.swift` looks like, with many changes in `NoteEntryView`:

```
1   import SwiftUI
2   import CoreData
3
4   struct ContentView: View {
5     @Environment(\.managedObjectContext) private var viewContext
6
7     @FetchRequest(
8       sortDescriptors: [NSSortDescriptor(keyPath: \NoteEntry.createdAt, a\
9   scending: true)], animation: .default)
10    private var noteEntries: FetchedResults<NoteEntry>
11
12
13    var body: some View {
14      NavigationView {
15        List {
16          ForEach(noteEntries) { noteEntry in
17            NoteEntryView(noteEntry: noteEntry)
18          }
19        }
20        .toolbar {
21          ToolbarItem {
22            Button(action: PersistenceController.shared.addNoteEntry) {
23              Label("Add Note", systemImage: "plus")
24            }
25          }
26        }
27        Text("Select a note")
28      }
```

```
29     }
30   }
31
32   private let itemFormatter: DateFormatter = {
33     let formatter = DateFormatter()
34     formatter.dateStyle = .short
35     formatter.timeStyle = .medium
36     return formatter
37   }()
38
39   struct NoteEntryView: View {
40     @ObservedObject var noteEntry: NoteEntry
41
42     @State private var titleInput: String = ""
43     @State private var contentInput: String = ""
44
45     var body: some View {
46       if let title = noteEntry.title,
47          let content = noteEntry.content,
48          let updatedAt = noteEntry.updatedAt {
49         NavigationLink {
50           VStack {
51             TextField("Title", text: $titleInput)
52               .onAppear() {
53                 self.titleInput = title
54               }
55               .onChange(of: titleInput) { oldTitle, newTitle in
56                 PersistenceController.shared.updateNoteEntry(
57                   noteEntry: noteEntry, title: newTitle, content: content\
58   Input)
59               }
60             TextEditor(text: $contentInput)
61               .onAppear() {
62                 self.contentInput = content
63               }
64               .onChange(of: contentInput) { oldContent, newContent in
65                 PersistenceController.shared.updateNoteEntry(
66                   noteEntry: noteEntry, title: titleInput, content: newCo\
67   ntent)
68               }
```

```
69              }
70          } label: {
71              Text(title)
72              Text(updatedAt, formatter: itemFormatter)
73          }
74        }
75    }
76  }
77
78
79  #Preview {
80    ContentView().environment(\.managedObjectContext, PersistenceControll\
81  er.preview.container.viewContext)
82  }
```

4. Run the app.

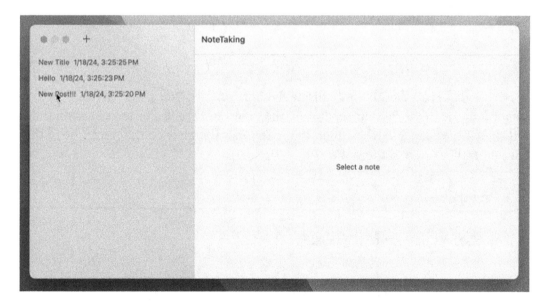

If you edit any of the inputs, you can see the updated data persists.

Deleting Note Entries

Previously, we removed the function related to deleting. Now, let's build our version of the delete functionality.

Adding Delete Button

We will make some changes to the label of the NoteEntryView. This label will have
a button to host the menu, which contains the button to delete a note entry.

1. In NoteEntryView, add a button to the label of NavigationLink.

```
1  } label: {
2    HStack {
3      Text(title)
4      Text(updatedAt, formatter: itemFormatter)
5      Spacer()
6      Button {
7        // TODO: add button action here
8      } label: {
9        Image(systemName: "minus.circle")
10     }.buttonStyle(.plain)
11   }
12 }
```

HStack() makes all the subviews displayed horizontally. Spacer() plays an
important role in the layout: separating the views next to it. For the views on the
left side of the Spacer(), they align to the left. For the ones on the right side of the
Spacer(), they align to the right.

2. Run the app.

A button shows up next to the label.

Tip: Wondering how I pick the icon `minus.circle`? It is from the app SF Symbols. SF Symbols is a library of iconography designed to integrate seamlessly with San Francisco, the system font for Apple platforms, hence the name SF. The library can be downloaded for free at SF Symbols[3]. We will talk about it more in Chapter 5.

3. Add the control to only show the delete button when hovering on the label.

We create a `@State` boolean variable `shouldShowDeleteButton` to keep the show/hide state. When the cursor hovers over the label, we set this variable to be true, otherwise, it is false. When it is true, we show the delete button, otherwise, we don't.

With the change, the `NoteEntryView` will look like this:

```
1  struct NoteEntryView: View {
2    @ObservedObject var noteEntry: NoteEntry
3
4    @State private var titleInput: String = ""
5    @State private var contentInput: String = ""
6
7    @State private var shouldShowDeleteButton = false
8
9    var body: some View {
10     if let title = noteEntry.title,
```

---
[3]https://developer.apple.com/sf-symbols/

```
11          let content = noteEntry.content,
12          let updatedAt = noteEntry.updatedAt {
13        NavigationLink {
14          VStack {
15            TextField("Title", text: $titleInput)
16              .onAppear() {
17                self.titleInput = title
18              }
19              .onChange(of: titleInput) { oldTitle, newTitle in
20                PersistenceController.shared.updateNoteEntry(
21                  noteEntry: noteEntry, title: newTitle, content: content\
22  Input)
23              }
24            TextEditor(text: $contentInput)
25              .onAppear() {
26                self.contentInput = content
27              }
28              .onChange(of: contentInput) { oldContent, newContent in
29                PersistenceController.shared.updateNoteEntry(
30                  noteEntry: noteEntry, title: titleInput, content: newCo\
31  ntent)
32              }
33          }
34        } label: {
35          HStack {
36            Text(title)
37            Text(updatedAt, formatter: itemFormatter)
38            Spacer()
39            if shouldShowDeleteButton {
40
41              Button {
42                // TODO: add button action here
43              } label: {
44                Image(systemName: "minus.circle")
45              }.buttonStyle(.plain)
46            }
47
48          }.onHover { isHover in
49            shouldShowDeleteButton = isHover
50          }
```

```
51              }
52          }
53      }
54  }
```

At this point, the delete button should only show up when the cursor hovers over the label. It makes the UI cleaner.

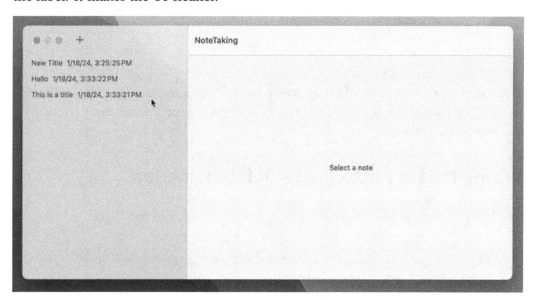

Deletion is an irreversible transaction. Once one entry is deleted from Core Data, it cannot be recovered. A good UX design for deletion is to have a dialog to confirm the deletion intention. It avoids accidental deletions. For this reason, let's add a confirmation dialog.

Adding Delete Function

Deleting a note is also transactional, so it can be placed into `PersistenceController` in `Persistence.swift`.

Add a function `deleteNoteEntry` in `PersistenceController`, next to `addNoteEntry` and `updateNoteEntry`.

```
1   func deleteNoteEntry(noteEntry: NoteEntry) {
2     let viewContext = container.viewContext
3     viewContext.delete(noteEntry)
4     do {
5       try viewContext.save()
6     } catch {
7       let nsError = error as NSError
8       fatalError("Unresolved error \(nsError), \(nsError.userInfo)")
9     }
10  }
```

This function ensures that when a NoteEntry is deleted, the changes are persisted to the Core Data store, preventing inconsistencies between the in-memory context and the persistent store.

Wiring Delete Button with Delete Function

The last step is to connect the dots between the function and the UI.

  1. In NoteEntryView, call the deleteNoteEntry inside delete button.

Add the following to the delete button handler.

```
1   PersistenceController.shared.deleteNoteEntry(noteEntry: noteEntry)
```

The logic for the button will look like this:

```
1   Button {
2     PersistenceController.shared.deleteNoteEntry(noteEntry: noteEntry)
3   } label: {
4     Image(systemName: "minus.circle")
5   }.buttonStyle(.plain)
```

  2. Run the app.

Now you should be able to delete a note by clicking the delete button and confirming.

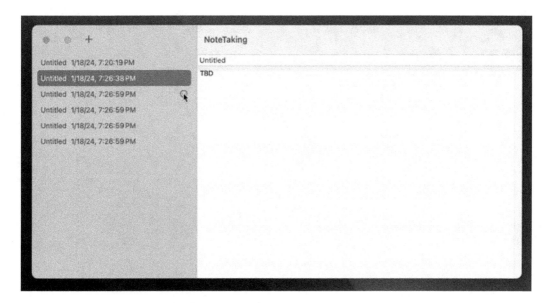

Fantastic! The basic functionality of a note-taking app is complete.

Final Clean-up

Removing the Entity Item

As we are not using the entity Item anymore, it is okay to remove the entity.

1. Simply click to select the entity Item, and hit the Delete key on the keyboard.

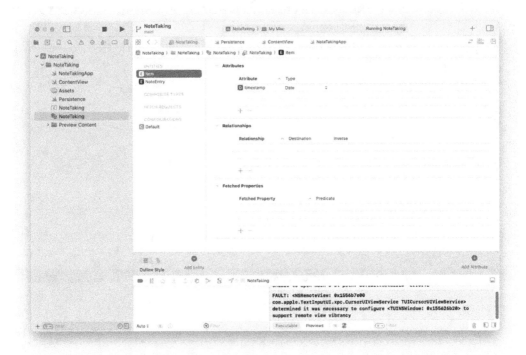

Once the entity is deleted, broken code may rise when you attempt to run the app, like the following:

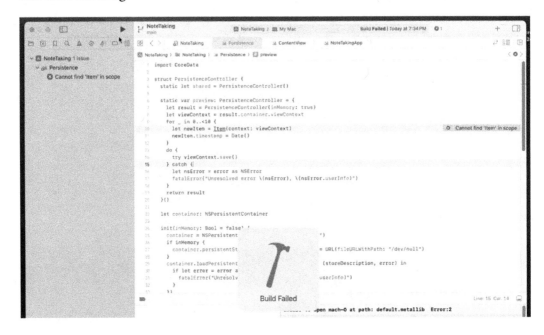

Use the error messages as hints to fix the issues.

In this case, PersistenceContainer is responsible to set up the Item mock data for the preview in canvas. Previously, it set up a set of 10 items. Here, we can similarly reuse and modify it for NoteEntry.

```
1   static var preview: PersistenceController = {
2     let result = PersistenceController(inMemory: true)
3     let viewContext = result.container.viewContext
4     for _ in 0..<10 {
5       let newNoteEntry = NoteEntry(context: viewContext)
6       newNoteEntry.createdAt = Date()
7       newNoteEntry.updatedAt = Date()
8       newNoteEntry.content = "(Content)"
9       newNoteEntry.title = "(title)"
10    }
11    do {
12      try viewContext.save()
13    } catch {
14      let nsError = error as NSError
15      fatalError("Unresolved error \(nsError), \(nsError.userInfo)")
16    }
17    return result
18  }()
```

2. Go to ContentView.swift, and hit Option+Command+P. It should update the Preview window. The mock data should be reflected.

3. Run the app.

The errors should disappear. The app should be built successfully.

DRY (Don't Repeat Yourself)

One of the engineering principles is Don't Repeat Yourself, short for DRY. It means reducing the code repetition.

As we've created multiple methods in `PersistenceContainer` to manage the transactions in Core Data, you can easily see some code repetition, as shown below:

```
1   import CoreData
2
3   struct PersistenceController {
4     static let shared = PersistenceController()
5
6     static var preview: PersistenceController = {
7       let result = PersistenceController(inMemory: true)
8       let viewContext = result.container.viewContext
9       for _ in 0..<10 {
```

```
10        let newNoteEntry = NoteEntry(context: viewContext)
11        newNoteEntry.createdAt = Date()
12        newNoteEntry.updatedAt = Date()
13        newNoteEntry.content = "(Content)"
14        newNoteEntry.title = "(title)"
15      }
16      do {
17        try viewContext.save()
18      } catch {
19        let nsError = error as NSError
20        fatalError("Unresolved error \(nsError), \(nsError.userInfo)")
21      }
22      return result
23    }()
24
25    let container: NSPersistentContainer
26
27    init(inMemory: Bool = false) {
28      container = NSPersistentContainer(name: "NoteTaking")
29      if inMemory {
30        container.persistentStoreDescriptions.first!.url = URL(fileURLWit\
31  hPath: "/dev/null")
32      }
33      container.loadPersistentStores(completionHandler: { (storeDescripti\
34  on, error) in
35        if let error = error as NSError? {
36          fatalError("Unresolved error \(error), \(error.userInfo)")
37        }
38      })
39      container.viewContext.automaticallyMergesChangesFromParent = true
40    }
41
42    func addNoteEntry() {
43      let viewContext = container.viewContext
44      let newNoteEntry = NoteEntry(context: viewContext)
45      newNoteEntry.createdAt = Date()
46      newNoteEntry.updatedAt = Date()
47      newNoteEntry.title = "Untitled"
48      newNoteEntry.content = "TBD"
49
```

```
50      do {
51        try viewContext.save()
52      } catch {
53        let nsError = error as NSError
54        fatalError("Unresolved error \(nsError), \(nsError.userInfo)")
55      }
56    }
57
58    func updateNoteEntry(noteEntry: NoteEntry, title:String, content: Str\
59  ing) {
60      let viewContext = container.viewContext
61      noteEntry.content = content
62      noteEntry.title = title
63      noteEntry.updatedAt = Date()
64
65      do {
66        try viewContext.save()
67      } catch {
68        let nsError = error as NSError
69        fatalError("Unresolved error \(nsError), \(nsError.userInfo)")
70      }
71    }
72
73    func deleteNoteEntry(noteEntry: NoteEntry) {
74      let viewContext = container.viewContext
75      viewContext.delete(noteEntry)
76      do {
77        try viewContext.save()
78      } catch {
79        let nsError = error as NSError
80        fatalError("Unresolved error \(nsError), \(nsError.userInfo)")
81      }
82    }
83  }
```

The chunk of code below is repeated three times in three different functions:

```
1  do {
2    try viewContext.save()
3  } catch {
4    let nsError = error as NSError
5    fatalError("Unresolved error \(nsError), \(nsError.userInfo)")
6  }
```

We can consolidate it into one.

1. Create a private function for saving viewContext.

Extract the common part into its own function, and it will look like this:

```
1  func save() {
2    let viewContext = container.viewContext
3    do {
4      try viewContext.save()
5    } catch {
6      let nsError = error as NSError
7      fatalError("Unresolved error \(nsError), \(nsError.userInfo)")
8    }
9  }
```

2. Update the caller functions to call save().

After the caller function has been updated, Persistence.swift will be significantly shorter, as shown below:

```
1  import CoreData
2
3  struct PersistenceController {
4    static let shared = PersistenceController()
5
6    static var preview: PersistenceController = {
7      let result = PersistenceController(inMemory: true)
8      let viewContext = result.container.viewContext
9      for _ in 0..<10 {
10       let newNoteEntry = NoteEntry(context: viewContext)
11       newNoteEntry.createdAt = Date()
```

```
12          newNoteEntry.updatedAt = Date()
13          newNoteEntry.content = "(Content)"
14          newNoteEntry.title = "(title)"
15        }
16      do {
17        try viewContext.save()
18      } catch {
19        let nsError = error as NSError
20        fatalError("Unresolved error \(nsError), \(nsError.userInfo)")
21      }
22      return result
23    }()
24
25    let container: NSPersistentContainer
26
27    init(inMemory: Bool = false) {
28      container = NSPersistentContainer(name: "NoteTaking")
29      if inMemory {
30        container.persistentStoreDescriptions.first!.url = URL(fileURLWit\
31 hPath: "/dev/null")
32      }
33      container.loadPersistentStores(completionHandler: { (storeDescripti\
34 on, error) in
35        if let error = error as NSError? {
36          fatalError("Unresolved error \(error), \(error.userInfo)")
37        }
38      })
39      container.viewContext.automaticallyMergesChangesFromParent = true
40    }
41
42    func save() {
43      let viewContext = container.viewContext
44      do {
45        try viewContext.save()
46      } catch {
47        let nsError = error as NSError
48        fatalError("Unresolved error \(nsError), \(nsError.userInfo)")
49      }
50    }
51
```

```
52    func addNoteEntry() {
53       let viewContext = container.viewContext
54       let newNoteEntry = NoteEntry(context: viewContext)
55       newNoteEntry.createdAt = Date()
56       newNoteEntry.updatedAt = Date()
57       newNoteEntry.title = "Untitled"
58       newNoteEntry.content = "TBD"
59
60       save()
61    }
62
63    func updateNoteEntry(noteEntry: NoteEntry, title:String, content: Str\
64  ing) {
65       let viewContext = container.viewContext
66       noteEntry.content = content
67       noteEntry.title = title
68       noteEntry.updatedAt = Date()
69
70       save()
71    }
72
73    func deleteNoteEntry(noteEntry: NoteEntry) {
74       let viewContext = container.viewContext
75       viewContext.delete(noteEntry)
76       save()
77    }
78  }
```

3. Run the app to confirm that it is working.

As you add more features to the app, there will be more scenarios like this. Refactor as you see fit.

Full Code

Congratulations! It has been quite a project, hasn't it? I hope you have been following along so far.

If not, don't worry! I've got you covered. You can always check out the entire codebase of this project on GitHub at https://github.com/higracehuang/NoteTaking-xcode15.

If you have any questions, please feel free to reach out by sending me a note at higracehuang@gmail.com.

Potential Future Development

Here are a few features that can be added to this project:

- **Delete Confirmation**: Add a confirmation dialog when the user attempts to delete a note.
- **Enhance the Look and Feel of the UI**: Improve the overall visual aesthetics and user experience.
- **Search Functionality**: Implement a search feature to allow users to quickly locate specific notes within the app.

For the Search Functionality, it may require querying Core Data based on specific keywords. It would be fun to play with.

Chapter 6: macOS Development and SwiftUI Basics

> "I hear and I forget. I see and I remember. I do and I understand." —
> Xunzi, Chinese Confucian philosopher

We have built 4 macOS projects together. What do you think? Do you feel more confident about building your ideas with macOS apps? If not, that's okay.

What Xunzi said is why I love the approach of learning by doing. You can gain understanding more effectively by doing things yourself. This is also why I structured the book this way: we start with building small projects, and then you can easily understand the purpose of each part. Now, we can learn about the concepts in detail.

In this chapter, we will go through the key concepts we have encountered in the projects, so you can understand why and how they are being used.

Views

Views are the basic building blocks in SwiftUI. Each view is a struct.

Let's use `ContentView.swift` as an example.

```
import SwiftUI

struct ContentView: View {
  var body: some View {
    Text("Hello, world!")
      .padding()
  }
}
```

`ContentView` is a view because it conforms to the `View` protocol. What is a `View` protocol? It defines a computed body property, which consists of the contents and behavior of the view.

We can categorize views into 2 types: **primitive views** and **container views**.

Primitive Views

The primitive views are the most basic building blocks in the more complex custom views. You may have seen and used these primitive views in the early chapters.

Here are some examples of primitive views:

- `Text()`
- `Image()`
- `Color()`
- `Shape()`
- `Spacer()`
- `Divider()`

Container Views

Container Views are for grouping and repeating views. Some are used for structuring and layout, for example, stack views and grid views. Others are used for more complex interfaces, such as lists and forms.

Here are some common Container Views:

- `Pane()`
- `VStack()`
- `HStack()`
- `ScrollView()`
- `NavigationView()`
- `List()`
- `Form()`
- `LazyVGrid()`
- `LazyHGrid()`

View Instance Methods

View instance methods are used to configure a view.

For example, if we would like to change the text color to red, we will add a method called `foregroundColor()`. To make the text bold, we will add the method `bold()`.

```
1   struct ContentView: View {
2     var body: some View {
3       Text("Hello, world!")
4         .foregroundColor(.red)
5         .bold()
6     }
7   }
```

Each kind of view has a rich set of applicable methods. They make SwiftUI very expressive.

Managing States In SwiftUI

SwiftUI provides a range of property wrappers to define how the data is observed, rendered, and transferred between views.

Property Wrappers

You must have seen the notations with @ in the projects, such as @State and @ObservedObject. They are property wrappers.

A proper wrapper is a type that wraps a given value to attach additional logic to it. What kind of additional logic is it? Let's talk about it one by one below.

@State

@State is a property wrapper. Its "additional logic" is to automatically make the view update when this state variable was changed.

Here is a code snippet we had in the project in Chapter 2.

```
1    struct NoteEntryView: View {
2      var noteEntry: NoteEntry
3
4      @State private var titleInput: String = ""
5      @State private var contentInput: String = ""
6
7      var body: some View {
8        if let title = noteEntry.title,
9           let content = noteEntry.content,
10          let updatedAt = noteEntry.updatedAt {
11         NavigationLink {
12           VStack {
13             TextField("Title", text: $titleInput)
14               .onAppear() {
15                 self.titleInput = title
16               }
17             TextEditor(text: $contentInput)
18               .onAppear() {
19                 self.contentInput = content
20               }
21           }
22         } label: {
23           Text(title)
24           Text(updatedAt, formatter: itemFormatter)
25         }
26       }
27     }
28   }
```

The two @State properties titleInput and contentInput are first assigned when noteEntry is passed into the view (onAppear). So a user can see the view updated with the values.

Also note that the @State properties are designed to contain simple values, such as booleans, integers, and strings. They are used to manage transients that only affect the UI, such as turning on a toggle button, or highlighting the state of a button. They are not designed to store complex data types, such as structs or classes.

Tip It is intended to keep the @State properties private. It ensures that they will only be mutated within the body of the view.

@Binding

A SwiftUI view may consist of multiple child views. If you want to notify the child views when a variable in the parent view changes, at the same time notify the parent view when child views change, you can use @Binding variables.

In addition, @Binding variables are either primitive values, such as integers and strings, or any Swift data type.

```
1   import SwiftUI
2
3   struct ContentView: View {
4     @State private var isSubAll:Bool = false
5
6     @State private var isSubNotif:Bool = false
7     @State private var isSubNews:Bool = false
8
9     var body: some View {
10      VStack {
11        Toggle("Subscribe All", isOn: $isSubAll)
12          .onChange(of: isSubAll) { isSubAll in
13            if isSubAll {
14              isSubNotif = true
15              isSubNews = true
16            }
17          }
18        DetailedSubscriptionView(
19          isSubNotif: $isSubNotif,
20          isSubNews: $isSubNews)
21      }.padding()
22    }
23  }
24
25  struct DetailedSubscriptionView: View {
26    @Binding var isSubNotif: Bool
27    @Binding var isSubNews: Bool
28    var body: some View {
29      VStack {
30        Toggle("Subscribe Notifications", isOn: $isSubNotif)
31        Toggle("Subscribe News", isOn: $isSubNews)
32      }
```

```
33    }
34  }
```

In this example above, when in the parent view (ContentView) the @State variable isSubAll changes to true, the isSubNotif and isSubNews will be changed to true. Because they are @Binding variables in the child view DetailedSubscriptionView, the toggles will change accordingly to be on.

Note that, when a @Binding variable is passed to a child view, this variable has a prefix $, for example, $isSubNotif. It is not an intrinsic value of the variable, such as Boolean. A binding value is like a vehicle that carries the state of the variable.

@EnvironmentObject

If you want a variable to be available for a view hierarchy (a tree of views), instead of passing the variable around, you can use an @EnvironmentObject.

```
1   import SwiftUI
2
3   class TweetSettings:ObservableObject {
4     @Published var fontColor: Color = .blue
5     @Published var picSize: CGFloat = 200
6   }
7
8   struct ContentView: View {
9     var tweetSettings = TweetSettings()
10    var body: some View {
11      VStack {
12        TweetView()
13        TweetView()
14        TweetView()
15      }.environmentObject(tweetSettings)
16    }
17  }
18
19  struct TweetView: View {
20    var body: some View {
21      ProfilePicView()
22      TweetText()
23    }
```

```
24    }
25
26    struct ProfilePicView: View {
27      @EnvironmentObject var tweetSettings:TweetSettings
28      var body: some View {
29        Image(systemName: "bird")
30          .resizable()
31          .frame(
32            width: tweetSettings.picSize,
33            height: tweetSettings.picSize)
34      }
35    }
36
37    struct TweetText: View {
38      @EnvironmentObject var tweetSettings:TweetSettings
39      var body: some View {
40        Text("Tweet Text")
41          .foregroundColor(tweetSettings.fontColor)
42          .onTapGesture {
43            tweetSettings.picSize = 150
44          }
45      }
46    }
```

In this example, the tweetSettings is passed as an environmentObject in ContentView.

When it is needed in the child views at any level, we just need to declare it as @EnvironmentObject to get access to this variable.

If any attribute of this object (for example, fontColor or picSize) is changed, any view that has declared tweetSettings as @EnvironmentObject will invalidate the view and cause it to re-render.

In the example above, when the user taps on the TweetText, picSize is changed to 150.

It will notify all the instances of ProfilePicView to change the size because in ProfilePicView declares TweetSettings as @EnvironmentObject.

You can see, for TweetText and ProfilePicView, we do not pass the tweetSettings around. Instead, we declare it as @EnvironmentObject in any view that needs it.

Note that, @EnvironmentObject needs to work with ObservableObject variables.

In another word, the model of @EnvironmentObject should conform to the ObservableObject protocol.

@Environment

@Environment variables manage system-managed environment values, such as color schemes, whether the app is running in the light or dark mode, Core Data's managed object context (as mentioned in Chapter 5), etc. They are key-value pairs, and keys are predefined.

```
 1  import SwiftUI
 2
 3  struct ContentView: View {
 4    @Environment(\.colorScheme) var colorScheme: ColorScheme
 5
 6    var body: some View {
 7      VStack {
 8        Text(colorScheme == .light ? "Light Mode" : "Dark Mode")
 9      }
10    }
11  }
```

The above code will check the system's predefined environment variable colorScheme.

If it is .light, it will output Light Mode. Otherwise, it outputs Dark Mode.

Besides colorScheme, there are many other variables, such as timeZone (the current time zone that views should use when handling dates).

For the complete environment variables, you can refer to SwiftUI EnvironmentValues[1].

@ObservedObject and @StateObject

If you want to pass an object to the view, and always get notified and re-render the view when the object changes, you can use @ObservedObject.

If you want to create an object inside the view, and re-render the view when the object changes, you can use @StateObject.

---

[1]https://developer.apple.com/documentation/swiftui/environmentvalues

@EnvironmentObject and @StateObject are very similar. To illustrate the difference between the two, this is an example slightly modified from the previous example with @EnvironmentObject.

It achieves the same result as before: when the TweetText is clicked, the size of the ProfilePicView changes. However, the @StateObject variable needs to be passed between views. (When we use the @EnvironmentObject variable, we only need to reference it when it is needed.)

```
1   class TweetSettings:ObservableObject {
2     @Published var fontColor: Color = .blue
3     @Published var picSize: CGFloat = 200
4   }
5
6   struct ContentView: View {
7     @StateObject var tweetSettings = TweetSettings()
8     var body: some View {
9       VStack {
10        TweetView(tweetSettings: tweetSettings)
11        TweetView(tweetSettings: tweetSettings)
12        TweetView(tweetSettings: tweetSettings)
13      }
14    }
15  }
16
17  struct TweetView: View {
18    @ObservedObject var tweetSettings:TweetSettings
19    var body: some View {
20      ProfilePicView(tweetSettings: tweetSettings)
21      TweetText(tweetSettings: tweetSettings)
22    }
23  }
24
25  struct ProfilePicView: View {
26    @ObservedObject var tweetSettings:TweetSettings
27    var body: some View {
28      Image(systemName: "bird")
29        .resizable()
30        .frame(
31          width: tweetSettings.picSize,
32          height: tweetSettings.picSize)
```

```
33      }
34    }
35
36    struct TweetText: View {
37      @ObservedObject var tweetSettings:TweetSettings
38      var body: some View {
39        Text("Tweet Text")
40          .foregroundColor(tweetSettings.fontColor)
41          .onTapGesture {
42            tweetSettings.picSize = 150
43          }
44      }
45    }
```

Note that both @EnvironmentObject and @StateObject need to work with the ObservableObject protocol and the ObservedObject property wrapper.

Core Data

Core Data is the framework to manage data model objects in the app. It is more than just SQLite data stores. It manages complex object graphs. The data models in Core Data are called entities. In your app execution, you can ask Core Data for filtered, sorted sets of entities for your needs. The saved data is persistent, meaning that after the device or the app restarts, data still exists.

In Chapter 5, we used Core Data to store the data locally. The capabilities of Core Data are far beyond managing local data. It can also sync data to multiple devices with CloudKit.

Many Apple built-in apps on iOS and macOS are believed to use Core Data for managing data locally on the device as well as syncing to iCloud, such as Contacts, Calendar, Reminders, and Notes.

If you are an Apple Watch user, you may be familiar with the Activity app where you can see the exciting progress your connections are making. This is a perfect example of using Core Data to selectively share data with recipients.

Figure 36. Apple built-in apps using Core Data: Notes, Calendar, Contacts, Reminders, and Activity (left to right)

Core Data is another extensive topic in Apple Development, and we won't cover it in detail in this book.

SF Symbols

SF Symbols is a library of iconography designed to integrate seamlessly with San Francisco, the system font for Apple platforms. It consists of over 5,000 symbols (in SF Symbols 5, at the time of writing). The latest version, SF Symbols 5, introduces expressive animations and improved tools for custom symbols.

SF Symbols was introduced in 2019. This has been a big game changer for iOS and macOS developers. In the past, developers had to rely on 3rd party SVG icons.

SF Symbols App

To use SF Symbols, you don't need to include anything in your app project. They are already part of the OS system. All you need to do is to look up the names and version compatibility on the macOS SF Symbols app.

It can be downloaded at https://developer.apple.com/sf-symbols/.

Figure 37. You can download SF Symbols on this website

How to Use SF Symbols

We have utilized SF Symbols multiple times in our projects.

Here is an example from the Windowless Screenshot app.

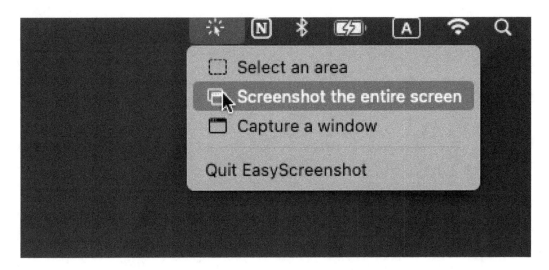

To acquire suitable icons, you only need to search in the SF Symbols app. For instance, for the window icon:

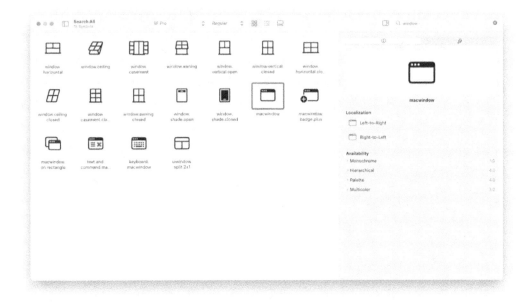

Figure 38. Details of the icon macwindow

1. Search for window in the search bar.
2. Find the preferred icon and click to view the details.
3. Verify its availability in the target version (or above) of your app.
4. If it is available for your target version, copy the string under the icon into the code. In this case, macwindow.

```swift
1   let windowImage = Image(systemName: "macwindow")
```

Chapter 7: Preparing For Launch

Before we package up the app for distribution, there are some crucial preparations to address, including:

- Minimum OS Version
- App Icon
- Localization

Adjusting the Minimum OS Version

During the development of RedacApp[1], I received feedback from customers stating that they couldn't install the app due to their macOS versions being lower than the app's target version.

Here's an example of the feedback I received:

---

[1]https://gracehuang.gumroad.com/l/redac

When we are making an app, a common goal is to distribute the app to the largest audience. Not all the customers have the macOS versions that we have. Chances are your customers are using lower macOS versions.

Go to Apple Icon -> About This Mac, you can find your macOS version.

In this example, it is 14.2.1.

MacBook Air

M1, 2020

Chip	Apple M1
Memory	8 GB
Serial number	C02GW411Q6L5
macOS	Sonoma 14.2.1

More Info...

Regulatory Certification
™ and © 1983–2023 Apple Inc.
All Rights Reserved.

To determine your app's minimum OS version, build your code with a lower OS target and observe which code breaks. Xcode will indicate which API is not available in which version. Based on the error messages, determine whether to refactor the code to support that version.

Locate the Deployment Info.

Select the project target in Xcode, and go to General. We can find the macOS version under Minimum Deployments.

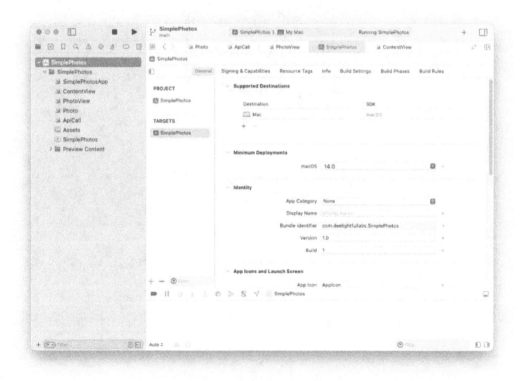

Figure 39. When we created the project, the Deployment Target was set to 12.2, which is the version of the Mac.

Lower the Deployment Target

Lower the macOS version gradually, and see whether you can still build the project successfully.

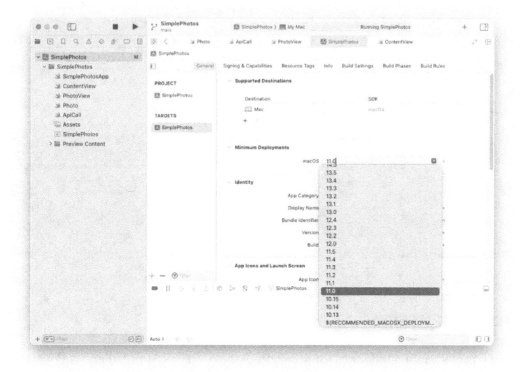

Figure 40. We lowered the Deployment Target to 11.0

App Icon

At this point, the icon for any app we have built in this book should look like the following:

Figure 41. No icon configured yet

Before shipping the app to customers, we need to design, create, and apply an icon for it.

App Icon Design

Apple provides the guidelines for app icon design[2]. Be sure to read and follow the guidelines while designing your app icons.

Here are a few ways to create app icons for your consideration:

1. Hire Professional Designers:

Professional designers can ensure top-notch quality and customized icons tailored to your app's branding. You can find them through word-of-mouth recommendations or by hiring freelance designers via platforms like Dribbble or Behance.

Pros:

- *High Quality:* Professional designers are skilled in creating visually appealing and high-quality icons.
- *Customization:* You can get a unique and customized icon tailored to your app's branding.
- *Expertise:* Designers understand design principles and can ensure your icon aligns with current trends.

Cons:

---

[2]https://developer.apple.com/design/human-interface-guidelines/app-icons

- *Cost:* Hiring professionals can be expensive, especially for small projects or individuals.
- *Time:* The design process may take time, impacting your app's development timeline.

2. Use AI Services:

Thanks to AI advancements, many icon-making services powered by AI have emerged. If you google "app icon AI," you can find plenty of such services.

Pros:

- *Speed:* AI services can generate icons quickly, reducing the time needed for design.
- *Affordability:* Some AI services are cost-effective compared to hiring a designer.
- *Variety:* AI tools often provide a range of design options to choose from.

Cons:

- *Lack of Customization:* AI-generated designs may lack the uniqueness and customization of professionally crafted icons.
- *Quality Concerns:* Results may vary, and the quality might not match that of a skilled designer.

3. Use Online Services:

You can also find task-based markets such as Fiverr and Upwork, where you can request icons based on your requirements.

Pros:

- *Affordable Options:* Online services may offer cost-effective solutions for icon design.
- *Quick Turnaround:* Many online platforms provide a fast turnaround for creating icons.
- *Accessibility:* Easy access for individuals who may not have design expertise.

Cons:

- *Quality Varies:* Similar to AI, the quality of designs may not be as high as those created by professionals.
- *Limited Customization:* Customization options might be limited compared to hiring a designer.

4. Do It Yourself:

With many tools and image assets available online, you can unleash your creativity and create your own icons.

Pros:

- *Full Control:* You have complete control over the design process.
- *Cost-Effective:* DIY is typically the most budget-friendly option.

Cons:

- *Skill Required:* Designing may require skills and tools that you may not possess.
- *Time-Consuming:* DIY design can be time-consuming, especially if you're learning as you go.

Consider your budget, timeline, and the importance of customization when choosing the method that best suits your needs.

Tip: You can always iterate on icons once you have the budget to improve them. If you don't have the budget yet, choose the low-cost approach.

In this book, we will use the logo below to illustrate the publishing process:

Figure 42. We will use the logo for the app.

Generating App Icon Assets

This step takes an image and transforms it into a set of images that the Xcode project can use.

In the Project navigator, click `Assets` > `AppIcon`; the different squares represent different sizes of icons for different contexts.

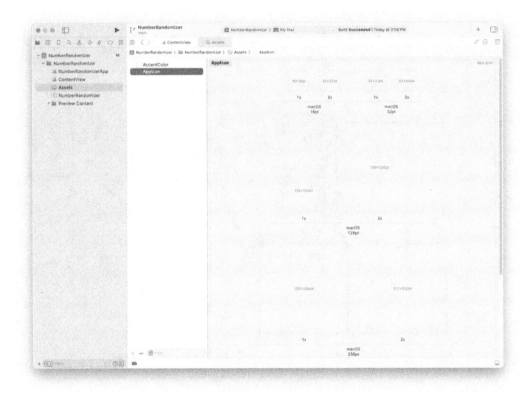

Figure 43. Assets

Once you have the app icon design, how can we create these images? We can manually resize the source image of the app icon, but it would be time-consuming.

Fortunately, many useful resources already exist to solve this problem:

- AppIcon.co[3]: generating flat icons with different sizes. Useful for iOS apps, not macOS apps.
- Image2Icon[4]: generating icons with rounded corners. Useful for macOS apps.

With the help of `Image2Icon`, I can generate an icon set, shown below.

---

[3]https://www.appicon.co
[4]https://img2icnsapp.com

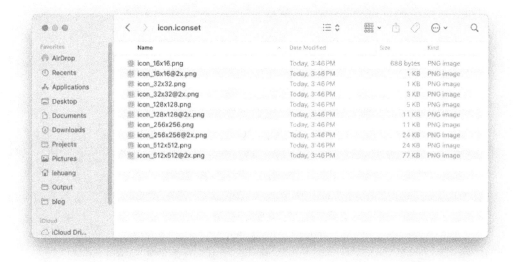

Figure 44. An Icon Set

Updating the Project

1. Drag the images into the designated positions

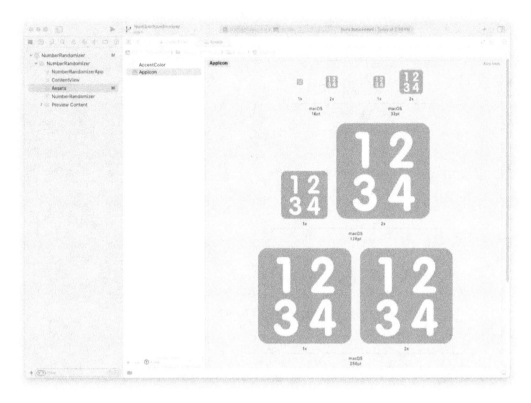

Figure 45. Updating the Assets

2. Navigate to Product in the top menu and select Clean Build Folder.

It is important to ensure that the icon is refreshed.

3. Run the app

Verify that the icon now appears in the dock.

Localization

Localization refers to the process of making your app support multiple languages, allowing it to display content in the user-specified language.

Typically, you initially develop the app in the language of your primary users, which, in our case, is English. If you wish to expand your target audience to include speakers of other languages, you can add support for additional languages, for example, Chinese, Korean, French, etc.

Tip Localization is optional. It is not necessary if your customer base only requires one language. Keep in mind that localization may involve a substantial effort and may require specific language skills, such as translation from one language to another. Whenever you introduce new features to your app, you need to consider localization for all the supported languages as well. Please consider this carefully before deciding to implement localization.

Thanks to the introduction of Xcode 5 at WWDC23, localization can now be easily accomplished using **String Catalogs**. Utilize a string catalog to localize and translate all your app's text through a visual editor right in Xcode. A string catalog *automatically* tracks all localizable strings from your code and consolidates your translations in one place.

Let's see how localization works in Xcode. We will use the project `NumberRandomizer` as an example.

Localize the App Content

1. Create a new `String Catalog` file.

Figure 46. Choose String Catalog

We can use the default name Localizable.

Figure 47. Create a new file called

After the file is created, no strings are generated yet.

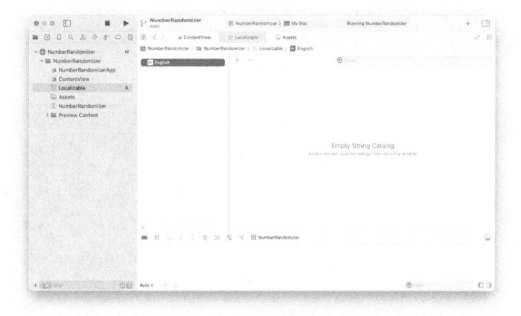

Figure 48. No Strings Generated

2. Run the app.

This step won't alter the app's behavior, but it prompts the app to recognize the new String Catalog file.

After completion, you'll observe new strings generated in the Localizable file. Xcode automatically detects the strings in your app and lists them here.

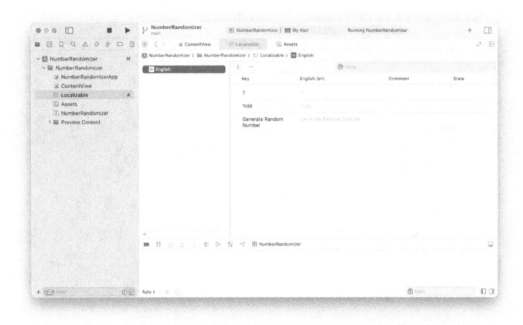

3. Add a new language to the App.

In this example, we'll translate the app into Simplified Chinese.

Click the + button, and select Chinese, Simplified

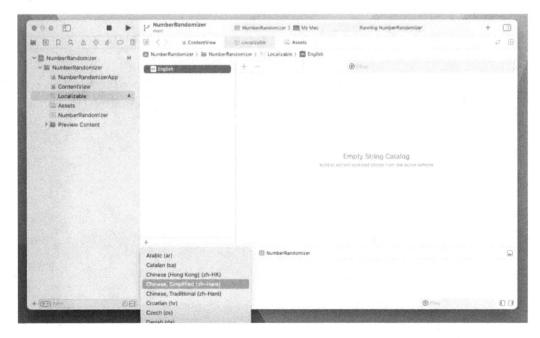

With the new language added, the strings are listed, but not translated yet.

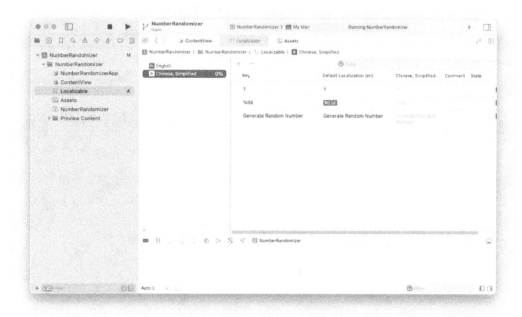

4. Translate the necessary strings in the new language (Simplified Chinese, in this example).

5. Edit the testing scheme to run the app with the new lanaguage.

Click Edit Scheme > Options > App Language > Choose Chinese, Simplified >
Close.

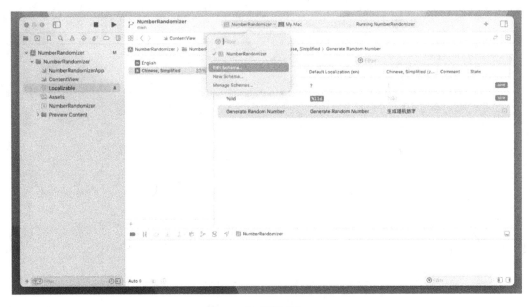

Figure 49. Edit Scheme

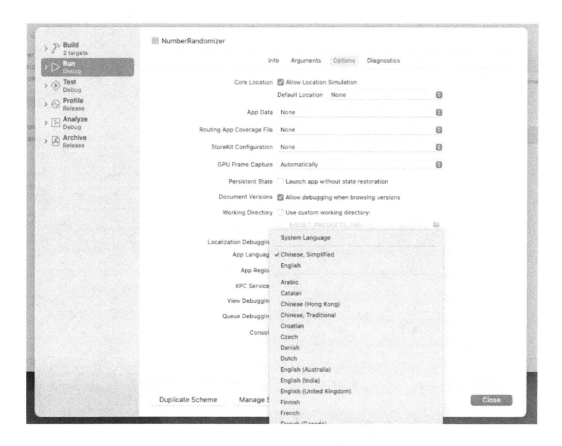

6. Run the app again.

Voila! The app is now in Chinese!

Chapter 8: App Store

App distribution refers to the process of making an app available for download and installation to your users.

Unlike iOS apps, which you can only distribute via the App Store, macOS apps offer two distribution options: self-distribution and the App Store.

Self-Distribution

Pros

1. **Flexibility**: You have more control over the distribution process and marketing strategies.
2. **Independence**: You are not dependent on the App Store's guidelines and restrictions.
3. **Direct Revenue**: You receive the full revenue from your app without any deductions.

Cons

1. **Responsibility**: You are responsible for making your app available for download and managing the entire distribution process.
2. **Marketing Effort**: Marketing and promoting your app become crucial, as you need to attract users on your own.
3. **Limited Reach**: Your app may have a smaller audience compared to the broader reach of the App Store.

App Store Distribution

Pros

1. **Wider Audience**: The App Store provides access to a large and diverse user base.
2. **Trust and Credibility**: Users often trust apps from the App Store due to Apple's review process.
3. **Easier Discovery**: Apps on the App Store are easily discoverable by users browsing the platform.

Cons

1. **Revenue Deduction**: The App Store deducts a percentage (around 30%) from your app revenue.
2. **Review Process**: The App Store has a rigorous and longer review process, leading to delays in app updates.
3. **Guideline Adherence**: Your app must adhere to Apple's guidelines, which may restrict certain functionalities.

Ultimately, the choice between self-distribution and the App Store depends on your priorities, resources, and marketing strategy. Some developers opt for a combination of both methods to leverage the benefits of each approach.

You can choose *one or both* of these distribution methods.

In this chapter and the next, we will discuss how to version your apps for release and explore both distribution approaches.

Version Management

Once we publish an app, we will add more features or fix bugs over time.

Version management is used to differentiate these incremental changes.

There are two definitions of versions in Xcode: **Version number** and **Build number**. Let's dive deep into how to define and use them for your app.

The `Version` and `Build` numbers are listed under (your build target) -> `General` -> `Identity`:

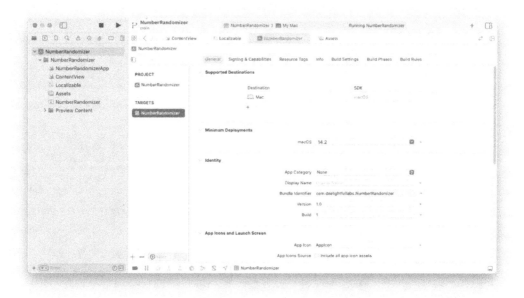

Version Numbers

A version number is assigned to each release of your app.

Apps on the App Store adhere to semantic versioning conventions with the format {major}.{minor}.{patch}. The major, minor, and patch components are numerical, incrementing with specific events.

- Major number increments for incompatible API changes.
- Minor number increments for backward-compatible functionality additions.
- Patch number increments for backward-compatible bug fixes.

For example, the version 1.0.0 represents the first release, while the version 2.0.1 represents a release that is incompatible with early releases.

The version you specify for the app will be visible in the App Store for customers.

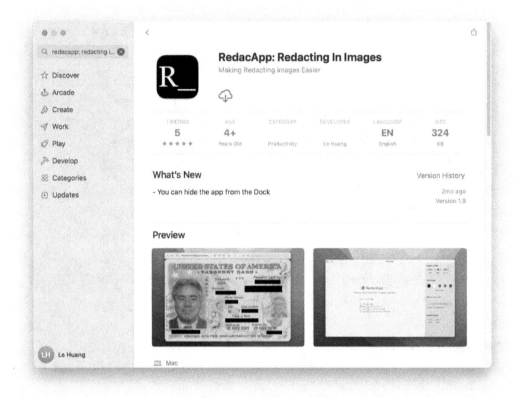

Figure 50. See the Version 1.9.0. It is published in App Store

Build Number

When preparing for a new release of your app, there may be issues to address, such as small bugs or string tweaks before the release. In such cases, where the app hasn't been released yet, you might not want to increment the version number. To distinguish these minor changes, you can use the Build number.

In Xcode, the version is defined under (your build target) -> General -> Identity -> Build. For example, 2.

Differences between iOS versioning and macOS versioning

- For **iOS apps**, you may re-use build numbers when submitting different versions:

  - Example: 1.0.0 (build 1), and 1.0.0 (build 2)

  - When you release 1.1.0, you don't need to increment the build number
  - Result: The app will be named 1.1.0 (build 1).

- For **macOS apps**, you must choose a new build number for every submission:

  - Example: 1.0.0 (build 1), and 1.0.0 (build 2)
  - When you release 1.1.0, you should increment the build number
  - Result: The app will be named 1.1.0 (build 3).

If the convention for macOS apps is violated, you may not be able to upload to App Connect properly.

Note that, this is something that people with prior experience in iOS development and the release cycle need to be aware of.

How to Use Build and Version

Now that you are familiar with what Version and Build are, here are the steps to follow:

1. Increment the Version number in Xcode.
2. Increment the Build number in Xcode.
3. (Optional) Git tag the code change.

As a best practice, we can also track the version changes in the Git history. For example:

```
git tag release-1.0.1
```

If you have a remote Git repo, you can follow the above command with this, to push it to the remote:

```
git push --tags
```

Good versioning is essential for clear communication, systematic issue tracking, and maintaining a transparent release history. It ensures users are informed about updates, facilitates feature rollouts, and builds trust through active maintenance and improvement efforts.

Uploading to App Store

Now, let's get ready to upload the app to App Store.

   1. Archive the app.

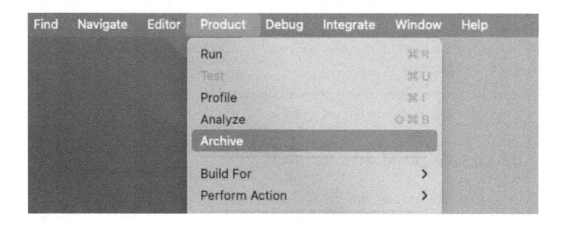

   2. Distribute the app.

Once the archive is ready, the following window will show up. Click Distribute App.

3. Upload to App Store

Tip: In case you don't want to create an archive but still want to see the window above, you can go to Xcode > Window > Organizer.

After everything is ready, request Apple for review.

When the app is approved, Apple will send you an email. Typically, it takes about 1 to 2 days. Then your app is in the App Store! Congratulations!

Chapter 9: Self-Distribution

When it comes to distributing your app, submitting to the App Store is not the only option—you can distribute the app yourself.

Notarizing

If you choose to distribute the installer independently, a key consideration is how to establish trust with your users for something you built. Apple provides a notary service for your app, ensuring its credibility.

The notarizing process is remarkably quick, typically taking only 2-3 minutes. Here's a simplified guide:

1. `Archive` the app, following a process similar to publishing on the App Store.
2. Select `Distribute App`.
3. Opt for `Direct Distribution`.

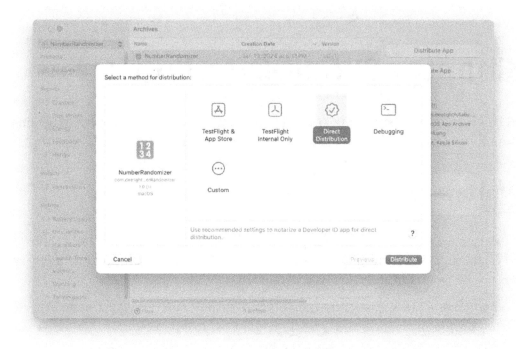

Figure 51. Choose

4. Wait for a notification in Xcode indicating that the app has been notarized. Your .app is now ready for distribution.

5. Click Export Notarized App to save the .app file to your preferred location.

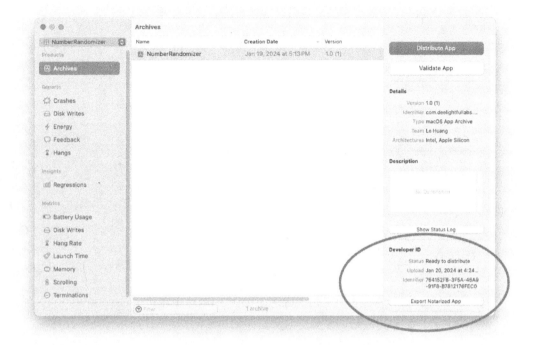

Figure 52. Ready to Distribute

Tip: Wondering why you need to pay Apple $99, even if you don't plan to sell your app on the App Store? The fee covers services such as the notary service and app reviews.

Generating Installer

For distribution, you can provide users with either a `.app` file or a `.dmg` installer. But what distinguishes these file types?

- A `.dmg` file is a copy of a virtual disk containing all the contents, including a `.app` file and perhaps a `README` file. It also facilitates the app installation process.
- A `.app` file is a self-contained entity with the necessary frameworks and libraries to function independently. Users can install the app by simply dragging the `.app` file to the Applications folder.

To generate a `.dmg` file, you can use the open-source script create-dmg[1].

---

[1]https://github.com/create-dmg/create-dmg

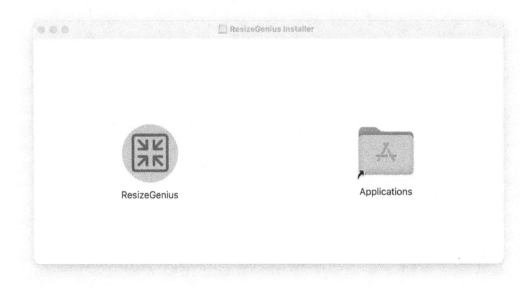

Figure 53. Example: ResizeGenius Installer

To streamline this process before each release, consider turning the script into a Shell script and saving it alongside the app source. For example, for NumberRandomizer:

```
create-dmg \
--volname "NumberRandomizer Installer" \
--window-pos 200 120 \
--window-size 800 400 \
--icon-size 100 \
--icon "NumberRandomizer.app" 200 190 \
--hide-extension "NumberRandomizer.app" \
--app-drop-link 600 185 \
"NumberRandomizer-Installer.dmg" \
"dist/"
```

Making App Available For Download

Once you have the .dmg installer ready, the next step is to make it available for download. Here are a few options to consider:

Option 1: Build a Website

Pros

- **Flexible Control**: Offers flexible control over the user experience.

Cons

- **Upfront and Recurring Costs**: Involves upfront and recurring costs and setup time, including purchasing a domain, cloud hosting, and setting up payment methods.
- **Traffic Challenge**: May face an initial challenge of generating traffic, necessitating efforts in SEO and backlinking.

Option 2: Use Creator Platforms (e.g., Gumroad)

Pros

- **No Upfront Costs**: No upfront costs; charges are per sale.

Cons

- **Self-Marketing Required**: Requires self-marketing to drive initial traffic.
- **Slightly Less Flexible**: Slightly less flexible compared to a custom-built website.

Option 3: Upload to Cloud Drive (e.g., Google Drive, Dropbox)

Pros

- **Cost-Effective**: No upfront or recurring costs.

Cons

- **Monetization Limitation**: Doesn't allow setting up payment for monetization.
- **Traffic Challenge**: Faces the challenge of generating initial traffic; requires external backlinking.

In my personal opinion, **Gumroad** is a preferred initial host. It offers free hosting for the app, facilitates the maintenance of a customer mailing list, and provides a mechanism for notifying users of updates. If the app gains traction, you might consider creating a dedicated website to enhance trust and optimize traffic through improved SEO.

Conclusion

In this book, we've learned how to make macOS apps, important concepts in SwiftUI and macOS development, and the steps to publish macOS apps.

As SwiftUI and macOS development keep evolving, I hope this book has given you a good starting point for your learning.

Contact the Author

If you have any questions, please feel free to reach out by sending me a note at higracehuang@gmail.com.

I frequently write about macOS development on Medium at https://medium.com/@imgracehuang. Feel free to follow me for updates.

Other Resources

For those seeking more advanced topics, here are valuable online resources:

- Apple Developer Documentation[1]: Great for API lookups.
- Stack Overflow[2]: Excellent for problem-solving and examples.
- AppCoda[3]: Offers SwiftUI tutorials and books.
- Hacking With Swift[4]: Provides concise articles about Swift.
- Swift With Majid[5]: Features insightful articles about Swift.
- Ray Wenderlich[6]: Offers outstanding tutorials about iOS and macOS development.

I hope you're feeling confident and excited to begin making your own macOS apps. I can't wait to see what you create!

---

[1]https://developer.apple.com/documentation/
[2]https://stackoverflow.com/
[3]https://www.appcoda.com/
[4]https://www.hackingwithswift.com/
[5]https://swiftwithmajid.com/
[6]https://www.raywenderlich.com/

About Author

Grace Huang was a software engineer at several big tech companies, including Amazon, Bloomberg. Grace co-founded a hardware / AI company Roxy. The product line was later acquired and the team joined Twitter. Since leaving Twitter, Grace has been focusing on writing and teaching.

Other technical books that Grace wrote:

- **Dynamic Trio**: Building Web Applications with React, Next.js & Tailwind
- **Nail A Coding Interview**: Six-Step Mental Framework
- **Code Reviews In Tech**: The Missing Guide
- **A Practical Guide to Writing a Software Technical Design Document**
- **Optimizing The 4% Rule**: How to Build, Backtest, and Manage a Financial Independence Portfolio

You can reach Grace at @imgracehuang[1] on X/Twitter.

---

[1]https://twitter.com/imgracehuang